Arden Wood #328

Library of Congress Control Number: 2001096769
Dickey, Adam Herbert, 1864-1925.
    Memoirs of Mary Baker Eddy / by Adam H. Dickey. --
1 st ed.
    p. cm.
    ISBN 0-930227-30-1

    1. Eddy, Mary Baker, 1821-1910. 2. Christian
Scientists--United States--Biography. 3. Christian
Science--History. I. Title.

BX6995.D45 2002   289.5'092
                            QBI01-201350

Published by
The Bookmark
Post Office Box 801143
Santa Clarita, California 91380

CONTENTS

Historical Note ... vii

Preface ... ix

Chapter I: The Summons to Duty ... 1

Chapter II: The Journey East ... 8

Chapter III: First Meeting with Mrs. Eddy ... 15

Chapter IV: "General Quarters" at Home ... 22

Chapter V: The Ideal of Orderliness and Regularity ... 30

Chapter VI: Generosity — A Lifelong Characteristic ... 39

Chapter VII: "Wit, Humor, and Enduring Vivacity"
Accuracy in Thought and Deed ... 42

Chapter VIII: Reluctance of Mrs. Eddy to Change Her
Writings in Response to Criticisms ... 48

Chapter IX: Changes in the Writings ... 51

Chapter X: The Twilight Hour
"Awake Thou That Sleepest" ... 56

Chapter XI: Leadership and Devotion to Her Cause ... 60

Chapter XII: Childhood Experiences ... 69

HISTORICAL NOTE

Adam H. Dickey was born in Toronto, Canada, in 1864. During the latter part of the 1800's the Dickey family moved to Missouri. Mr. Dickey became interested in Christian Science after he witnessed its healing effects. Both he and his wife, Lillian S. Dickey, entered the healing ministry in Kansas City, Missouri, and became listed as Christian Science practitioners in *The Christian Science Journal* in 1900. Two years later they went through Normal Class with Edward A. Kimball, and became teachers of Christian Science. Soon afterwards they opened the Intra-State Christian Science Institute, with offices in both New York City and Kansas City.

In February, 1908, Mr. Dickey was called to Chestnut Hill, Massachusetts, to serve Mary Baker Eddy in various capacities. He was the last confidential secretary to join her staff before she passed on in December, 1910.

Mrs. Eddy appointed Mr. Dickey to be one of the five Directors of The Mother Church in Boston, a position he held for fourteen years. He also served as Treasurer of The Mother Church and as a Trustee under the Will of Mary Baker Eddy.

While Mr. Dickey was at Chestnut Hill, Mrs. Eddy secured a promise from him under oath that he would write a history about his years of service with her. The real purpose of such a history was to show the cause of Mrs. Eddy's death to be mental murder. Sixteen years later he wrote these memoirs from records made while he was with her. He did not live to finish the book nor to elaborate on Mrs. Eddy's urgent and specific request. His widow published the unfinished manuscript in 1927, a year after his death, and copies were distributed to Christian Scientists whom Mr. Dickey had taught.

Mrs. Dickey did not consult the Board of Directors of The Mother Church concerning the publication of these memoirs. The Directors declared upon reading it that its issuance was a grave mistake. They insisted that Mrs. Dickey stop distribution of the book and withdraw every copy that had been distributed. They claimed that Mr. Dickey could have complied with Mrs. Eddy's request by writing his memoirs for the church archives. The Board soon acquired the copyright to the book, the Dickey pupils were requested to turn in their copies to The Mother Church, and the book was promptly buried in the archives.

A few printed and photostated copies remained in circulation, however, and copies of the book were quietly passed from hand to hand among Christian Scientists for many years. In 1980, it was once again put into print and so made available to the public. This printing is a copy of the 1927 publication, with the spelling and capitalization left as it was in the original. The three items in brackets ([-]) have been inserted by the publisher.

This book is unique among the many memoirs and biographies about Mrs. Eddy in that she requested Mr. Dickey to write it. Indeed, she made him promise to do so. This request was most unusual. There are records to show that she discouraged students from writing about her. It would appear that she opposed a human account of her life by those who did not fully understand her or her discovery. But in the case of Mr. Dickey, she must have considered him sufficiently discerning that he could go beneath the surface of events and detect the real cause of her passing on. Unfortunately, he left the book unfinished, and therefore he did not fulfill his promise to relate her death to mental assassination. Even so, these memoirs are invaluable as a historical document, for they tell of the many obstacles that Mrs. Eddy faced in working to secure the future of her beloved Cause. Although Mr. Dickey's book falls short of its original goal, it gives fascinating insights into the many aspects of Mrs. Eddy's last two years.

PREFACE

Writing a book always seemed to me a tremendous task. A book in a way looks so formidable, and the thought of sitting down in the endeavor to write one has ever been almost appalling to me. Perhaps if I should set aside the thought of book writing and look upon it merely as recording some of the incidents in the life and experience of our Leader, Mary Baker Eddy, that I know must be preserved, the task would seem lighter. If, however, what I have to say is properly recorded, I know that it will be read and perhaps consulted or referred to for many years to come. As long as there is an interest in the life and works of Mary Baker Eddy, the memoirs of one who lived in her home as her private secretary for nearly three years should be at least interesting. To many of those who read this book I am known personally, and to many others I am known by name; but in years to come this will not be the case, and I feel that the reader who is expected to accept as facts the things which I shall here relate will have a right to know who it is that is asking him to accept his statements regarding the life of the greatest benefactor to humanity that has lived since the time of Jesus of Nazareth.

Concerning Mary Magdalene Jesus said, "Wheresoever this gospel shall be preached in the whole world, there shall also this, that this woman hath done, be told for a memorial of her." (Matt. 26:13) I therefore feel that the author of this book will necessarily come in for some share of publicity. Then if the reader of the present day will pardon some reference to myself, I will make a few statements for the benefit of future readers who may have no means of acquaintance with the author other than what is said here.

I was born in Toronto, Canada, in the year 1864, the second son in a family of nine children, six boys and three girls. My father's name was Nathaniel Dickey, and he was a native of the town of Lisburn, Ireland, a devout and consecrated Christian of the early days. My great-grandfather's name was also Nathaniel Dickey. His forebears were natives of Scotland and in the time of King James were part of a colony which went to settle in the north of Ireland, having been given a grant of land by the King. He was one of the signers of a petition asking for lay representation in the Presbyterian Church and was dismissed from membership for daring to question church authority. He was converted to Methodism under John Wesley and accompanied Wesley for a considerable time during his tour of Ireland. He became a class leader and a lay preacher in the Methodist Church.

My father came to the United States in the year 1848, and afterward went to Toronto, Canada, where he engaged in the iron-foundry business. I never knew a better man than my father. He was clean in thought and in language. I never knew him to utter even a slang expression. His life was one of uprightness and purity and he was admired and respected by all who knew him. After he passed on his children found in his diary under the date of August 7, 1859, the following entry, which gives a better insight into my father's character than I ever could:

August 7th, 1859.

In the name of the Father & of the Son & of the Holy Gost I thus solemly inter into a covenant with my Creator & Redeemer, having for its end the Glory of God & the salvation of my soul.

And that I may be directed aright at this time, I Beseech Thee Heavenly Father to grant me the enlightening influences of thy Holy Spirit, Both to dictate the course most proper to be

*pursued & to strengthen me that I may be kept
faithful in the discharge of the following
duties, for Jesus sake, Amen.—
1st   I give myselfe Body Soul & Spirit into
the hands of my Creator to be used as Gods
will may direct,
2nd   That I will at least twice every day
approach him in prayer for the pardon of my
sins & full developement of my Christian character,
3rd   That I will at least once each day read &
endevour to understand some portion of his
holy word,
4th   That I will endevour to become recon-
ciled to any with whome I may be at variance
and make restitution to such as I may have in
any way injured . . .
5th   That in all matters of doubt or un-
certainty I will keep the example of Jesus before me & endevour to act according to my
knowledge of his will,
6th   That I will keep a journal in which to
record my observations & reflections, For it is
evident I have lost much by not having kept
any record of the various events of my life.*

My mother was a descendant of George Soule who came
over in the "Mayflower." Her mother, Sarah Ann Soule, married
Robert Simpson, a young Englishman, who settled in Ontario,
Canada. On her mother's side she was a descendant of Revolu-
tionary stock and also of those who for many years fought in the
early American colonial wars. She was the mother of nine children, of whom I was the second. My mother was scrupulously

honest and frank. I never knew her to deceive one of her own children, even in the many trifling ways wherein parents sometimes think it best to misinform their children. The Bible was an open book in our household, and the custom of family prayer and Bible reading, established in early years, remained with our family until the children were grown and had left home. I have always had a fondness for the Bible and while still very young attached myself to the Methodist Church, continuing active in young people's meetings and class work until I came into Christian Science.

A Commission from Mrs. Eddy

It was the custom of our Leader to lie down for an hour each afternoon and rest. Sometimes she would fall asleep, and upon awakening would seem mentally refreshed after her labors of the day. Many times when important matters were under consideration she would, on awakening from these short naps, come to a quick determination as to the right method to pursue in whatever she had in hand.

On Tuesday, August 25, 1908, my bell rang, calling me to Mrs. Eddy's apartment. When I entered her study she was lying on the lounge where she usually took her rest. Requesting Mrs. Sargent, Mr. Frye, and a third student to leave the room, she beckoned me to approach. She extended her hand to me, took mine in both of hers, and asked in a deep, earnest voice, "Mr. Dickey, I want you to promise me something, will you?

I said, "Yes, Mother, I certainly will."

"Well," she continued, "if I should ever leave here — do you know what I mean by that?"

"Yes, Mother."

"If I should ever leave here," she repeated, "will you promise me that you will write a history of what has transpired in your experiences with me, and say that I was mentally murdered?"

I answered, "Yes, Mother, I will."

"Now, Mr. Dickey, do not let anything interfere with your keeping this promise. Will you swear to me before God that you will not fail to carry out my wish?"

I raised by right hand and said, "Mother, I swear before God that I will do what you request of me, namely, write a history of what I have seen, and heard from your lips, concerning your life."

"That will do, dear. I know now that you will not fail me."

Her whole demeanor was one of solemn intensity, and there was an eagerness in her voice and manner such as I seldom saw.

I returned to my room and pondered deeply over what she had said. In a few minutes one of the workers and Mrs. Sargent brought me a sealed envelope. In it was a penciled note reiterating the statement that she had made in our conversation of a short time before.

I knew that Mrs. Eddy had an aversion to having her private life spread before the public. I knew also that on several occasions the proposition had been made to her by others to write a history of her life and experiences, all of which she firmly declined to consider. Her reply to proposals of this kind was, "The time has not yet come for my history to be written. The person to whom this important work should be entrusted is not here yet and I will not give my consent to its being done at this time." This was the nature of the reply she invariably made whenever some of her loving students proposed to her that her life history should be written.

In the request she had just made of me, I felt that Mrs. Eddy did not intend me to write a detailed history of her life; but I know she wanted the incidents and the circumstances of which I was a witness to be given to the world. I also felt then, and feel now, that there is no alternative but for me to put on record the experiences and incidents which transpired in her life of which I was an eyewitness, and which she related to me with her own lips.

I have hesitated to begin the narration of these incidents, but have always been determined in my own mind that it should be done, and have felt that when the time came, I should have no difficulty in proceeding.

Sixteen years have come and gone since this promise was made. A great many changes have taken place in our Movement, but the Cause has still gone on and flourished in spite of the attacks made upon it. Because of the extremely personal nature of what I shall be compelled to write I still have a strong reluctance to record my memories, although I know this hesitancy is not my own thought, but comes from without. The recollection of my solemn promise impels me to take up this work now at this late date and turn back to the record I made while in our Leader's home of the events that are set forth. I am making use of nothing that is not authentic, and although I am unable to include more than a part of what I had written down, I am confident that there is sufficient to carry out the obligation which our Leader placed upon me.

ADAM H. DICKEY

Chapter I

THE SUMMONS TO DUTY

During the year 1907, while serving as First Reader in First Church of Christ, Scientist, Kansas City, Missouri, I received a call from a gentleman from Boston, who spent a few hours, Sunday afternoon, in our home. He informed me of the nature of his errand in Kansas City, which was to the effect that he was looking for people to go to Concord, New Hampshire, to live in the home of Mrs. Eddy and there to serve her in different capacities.

He explained to me that it was difficult for our Leader to find suitable persons to assist in her household. When she needed a personal maid, there were always plenty of volunteers, but very few who could pass the requirements. The same situation existed in regard to other work in the household, — difficulty in finding persons to do the necessary cooking, serving, and other general tasks.

I was informed then, that Mrs. Eddy had quite a large household and that those serving in any capacity in her home came under a line of malpractice that existed nowhere else on earth. The difficulty of discovering people who would meet the requirements and who possessed the necessary qualifications for performing this work for our Leader made it necessary for the Directors, acting under Mrs. Eddy's instruction, to appoint a committee whose sole purpose was to scour the country, if need be, in order to find suitable persons. Our Leader in her great work for humanity found it necessary that her time and thought be fully given to the work in hand, and that she should not be occupied or annoyed with petty details of household management. The members of this committee, usually three in number, of which my caller was at that time the traveling representative, interviewed many people in their effort to find any who were qualified to perform this work. They must be willing to leave homes and friends and take up their residence in the home of our Leader. ("And every one that hath forsaken houses, or brethren, or sisters, or father, or mother, or wife, or children, or lands, for my name's sake, shall receive an hundredfold, and shall inherit everlasting life." Matt. 19:29)

Our Leader was very strict in her requirements. For instance, if one had formerly suffered from a belief that had incapacitated him, even though he had been healed and restored apparently to perfect health, she did not want such a person in her house. Her reason for this has already been alluded to, — that as soon as the individual entered Mrs. Eddy's employ he came under a certain malicious mental malpractice that he had never encountered before, and our Leader was unwilling to subject anybody to this trial, who might be liable to a relapse or return of a diseased belief.

One might easily ask the question, why should not Mrs. Eddy immediately heal one of the old belief in case it should return? Very true, Mrs. Eddy could have done so, but healing the sick in Christian Science is not a pastime, nor merely a wish, unaccompanied by earnest effort, as every practitioner can testify. It requires special time and attention, and our Leader had other things to do than to heal sick people who had come down under such claims in her home. People were not invited to Mrs. Eddy's house for their own improvement. They were invited there to work, and what she required of them was not that they should work for themselves, but that they should work for her and for the Cause of Christian Science. Therefore, experience taught her that it was wiser and better at the outset to decline to receive people who were liable in any way to an attack from mortal mind, than to accept such individuals and have them struggling with a belief of illness after they had arrived at her home.

Hence it was incumbent on the committee, who had charge
of this work, to investigate thoroughly those whom they were considering for positions of this kind and ascertain, before employing
them, that they would meet all the requirements. Sometimes such
an investigation had to be made with the prospective worker un-
aware of why he was being questioned, and this was not always a
very easy task.

In his conversation with me my visitor frankly told me what
Mrs. Eddy's requirements were and asked me if I knew of any
Christian Scientist whom I thought would successfully pass such
an investigation as would have to be made. My reply at that time
was, "I know many people who would be glad to go there, but I
know of no one at present that I think would be good enough to go
into our Leader's home and serve her in the capacity of personal
maid," the position which he was seeking to fill at that time.

Who would not have jumped at the opportunity to go to
Mrs. Eddy's home and work for her! Hundreds would offer themselves for this position if they had only known when it was open.
One difficulty in connection with this series of investigations was
that many people upon learning that there was a prospect, however
remote, of serving Mrs. Eddy took pains to conceal from the committee the fact that they were subject sometimes to attacks from
mortal mind. They felt that if they could only get under our Leader's
roof ,they could thereafter bask in the sunshine of her smile and
forever be beyond any possibility of an evil attack. Teachers many
times eagerly recommended their own students with the thought
that it would be quite a distinction to have a student serving
our Leader. How little they really knew of the situation may be
estimated from what has already been said of the claims of malicious attack to which the workers were subjected.

Every one who was in Mrs. Eddy's home was there because of his ability to work and to perform the tasks that were set
for him. Many people seemed to be inspired with a belief that there

could be no pleasanter occupation in the world than to work for Mrs. Eddy. They failed to realize that what Mrs. Eddy wanted and actually required of those about her was the mental support which she found necessary to receive from students in order that she might be uninterrupted in her work for her Cause and for mankind. Mrs. Eddy was at the head of a great Movement, a Church that had grown up under divine direction and was designed, eventually, to destroy all evil and bring to suffering humanity a remedy for every form of sickness and sin. The same form of evil that attacked the work of Jesus and cried out, "What have we to do with thee, thou Jesus of Nazareth? art thou come to destroy us?" (Mark 1:24), was by no means lacking in connection with Mrs. Eddy's experience. She was in a position somewhat similar to that of the general of a large army, who is fighting for its existence. The attacks of the enemy would be made, if possible, on the leader of the defending army. Usually in such cases the commanding officer occupies a safe point of vantage far in the rear of his fighting troops, from which he can issue orders and send forth his commands, unmolested and unthreatened by the attacking forces. In times gone by, the general of an army was required to be in the front of the battle leading his men, but in such events he was invariably surrounded by an able bodyguard sufficient to protect him from every possible attack. The members of this bodyguard were not weaklings, nor soldiers who had been disabled and had not regained their full strength. He was surrounded by the very flower of the army. The best fighters and most capable workers were at his elbow constantly.

Mrs. Eddy was in much the same position in the leadership of this Movement. She could occupy no convenient retreat from which to direct the movements of her slender battalions. She must be in the front rank in the thick of battle every day, and she needed to be surrounded by the best workers she could find, who virtually acted as a bodyguard and a protection for her in order that she might be able to give her undivided attention to the work necessary to properly safeguard her Church. Thus it was that every person who went to Mrs. Eddy's home had to be tried and tested before he assumed his duties.

The committee member's visit with me at Kansas City brought the first intimation I had ever had that such precaution was necessary, or indeed, that Mrs. Eddy required reinforcement in her home. I had always imagined that Mrs. Eddy lived quietly, as any other elderly woman would live, surrounded by comforts and luxuries, and by those friends whom she wished to invite to share her home with her. I had no idea that she was constantly besieged by all the forces of evil and that she had to be in the front line of battle, day and night, throughout all the years of her leadership. It was very interesting to me to learn how these things were being done. After my guest's departure, we corresponded occasionally, and sometimes he would call me on the telephone when passing through the city. Each time he would ask me if I had been able to think of anybody who would fill the requirements. Later on he was looking for someone to assist with the housework. Again, a cook was needed or someone for work of that sort, but always I was impressed by the fact that it was difficult to obtain such material as that for which he was looking.

Shortly after these interviews, I visited Boston, in June of 1907, to attend the communion service and Annual Meeting. Here again I met the student who had called upon me in the west, and for the first time learned that while he was quizzing me about other people, who might be employed to work for Mrs. Eddy, he was quietly sizing me up as a possible choice for an assistant in Mrs. Eddy's home in connection with secretarial work. When in Boston on this occasion I was invited to step into the Treasurer's office, which at that time was in The Mother Church, and there I was interviewed by a committee of three. They questioned me quite closely with regard to my own work and the length of time I had been in Science, and what I felt I had accomplished, and then asked me if I would be willing to respond to a call from the Directors, in case they should see fit to invite me to work in Mrs. Eddy's home. I told them I had no higher aim in life than to be of service to Mrs. Eddy and the Cause of Christian Science, and that if they needed somebody to shovel the snow off her front sidewalk, I would drop everything else and give all my time to her service in any capacity whatever. I remember my reference to shoveling snow brought forth a little laugh, and one of the members of the committee remarked that they didn't seem to have much difficulty in getting people to shovel snow, but it was with regard to work of an entirely different nature that they were concerned. They asked me if I could use a typewriter and I replied in the affirmative. This interview was, of course, a private one, and I dismissed the subject when it was over, and thought no more of it until my first questioner reappeared in Kansas City, January 26, 1908. He was still looking for the household workers for Mrs. Eddy and had been traveling over the country quite a good deal with that end in view.

On January 29, 1908, I received a special delivery registered letter from the Board of Directors of The Mother Church, which read as follows:

January 26, 1908

MR. ADAM H. DICKEY, C.S.B.,
The New York,
12th & Paseo,
Kansas City, Mo.

Dear Brother:
· The Directors hereby extend to you a loving call to serve our beloved Leader, the Rev. Mary Baker Eddy, according to the terms of the By-law Article XXII, Sect. 10 of the Church Manual.

6

If you will come sooner than the ten days, it will be very much appreciated.

As soon as you can after receiving this letter, will you please telegraph me at what time you will be in Boston? And upon your arrival, call me by telephone at Back Bay 1470 between the hours of 8:00 and 12:00 A.M. and 1:00 and 5:00 P.M. and at Back Bay 1506 at other times.

Very sincerely yours,
WILLIAM B. JOHNSON,
Secretary.

Immediately I replied that I would leave Kansas City for Boston the following Monday.

My sense of duty in connection with this call prompted me to say nothing to anyone about it. At the time, I was serving as First Reader of First Church of Christ, Scientist, in Kansas City, Missouri, and to sever my connection with church duties, to abandon suddenly a large practice without giving some reasonable explanation for my departure and continued absence, was not an easy task. The By-law referred to in the letter stated that I must serve for one year, and I felt it would be wiser not to announce my destination before leaving, but to explain my absence after I had reached Boston. Arriving at this conclusion, I packed my trunk with the thought of being absent for a year and took my departure.

Chapter II

THE JOURNEY EAST

On Monday, February 2, 1908, I left Kansas City bound for Boston, with high expectations of the wonderful experiences which lay before me. I arrived in Chicago the following morning. There I had some time to spare, and having been unable to purchase a copy of the latest *Manual* in Kansas City, before leaving, I visited the Reading Room, a magnificently furnished apartment on the top floor of a building on South Michigan Ave. I did not make myself known to the Librarian, but, observing a consignment of new *Manuals* which had just arrived, I purchased one and turned to Article XXII, Section 11. Somewhat to my surprise I saw that the wording had been changed, so that the person accepting the call, instead of remaining with Mrs. Eddy for one year, unless she requested otherwise, the By-law read, should remain for three years. [This By-law was changed in 1905 in the 49th edition of the *Church Manual*. It is now numbered Section 2.]

This furnished me with much food for thought, but having put my hand to the plow, I could not turn back. Besides, the thought of being chosen to serve the Leader of the Christian Science Movement for one year or a dozen seemed such a precious opportunity to me that even the prospect of being absent from my home for three years could offer no possible deterrent to me on this momentous trip.

I had much time to ponder the situation as the train carried me eastward. Mrs. Eddy I had seen but once, on July 4, 1907, when she invited the members of The Mother Church to visit her at Pleasant View, in Concord, New Hampshire, and now I was to see

8

her again, and perhaps enter her household and serve her in some capacity, I did not know what. My thoughts were buoyant and hopeful and I felt that no greater blessing could fall to me than to receive such a call.

The country was covered with snow, which fell during all the trip. Trains were delayed and traffic generally interfered with because of the constant snowfall. Instead of reaching Boston at three o'clock in the afternoon, the train pulled into the station at eleven in the evening.

In accordance with instructions in the letter from Mr. William B. Johnson, Secretary of the Board of Directors, I called him by telephone at his home. He directed me to a hotel and said he would call for me at 6:30 the next morning, and asked if I could be ready. At the appointed hour I was on hand, although it was still dark. Mr. Johnson had inquired at what hour the first street car left for Chestnut Hill, and we boarded it as it passed the hotel. At Lake Street on Commonwealth Avenue a horse and sleigh from a nearby livery stable met us, and we were drawn through heaps of snow until we arrived at Mrs. Eddy's front door. Mr. Johnson alighted with me and we were admitted to the home. The family was at breakfast when we arrived. Mr. Frye, who sat at the head of the table and assumed the position of host, invited Mr. Johnson to breakfast with us, but he declined and returned immediately to his home.

After meeting Mr. Frye, I was introduced to Mrs. Laura Sargent, whom I already knew, and to three other members of the household including the gentleman who was serving temporarily as secretary to Mrs. Eddy. After breakfast he told me many things about Mrs. Eddy's household that were new and interesting to me. In fact, he was the only one who ventured to talk to me concerning my sudden entrance into the household, and what I might expect as a result. I learned afterward the reason for the reticence that was assumed by the other members of the household. I was a comparative stranger, little known to any of them. They knew I had been sent for on Mrs. Eddy's call. They also were aware that I would have to pass the customary examination, through which everyone passed who was brought to Mrs. Eddy's home with the expectation of serving her. None of them knew whether I would remain after the interview long enough to unpack my valise, or whether I would remain for three years. Many of the people who came to our Leader's home scarcely crossed the threshold, while others were interviewed by Mrs. Eddy and remained perhaps a day or two, and when she saw their services were not to be desired, they were allowed to depart and return home.

During this first breakfast, conversation turned on my trip eastward, and I learned that I had been expected to arrive the day before, Mrs. Eddy having been caused some concern over the delay. They asked me in rather a pointed way if we had encountered much snow on the trip. I explained that the whole country was covered with a blanket of snow, which was responsible for my delay. Mr. Frye at once said, "We must tell Mother about that." I wondered at the time what there was in that little discussion that could interest Mrs. Eddy. I afterward learned that she had an aversion to heavy snowfalls, and that they were the damaging results of error and ought not to be tolerated. It seems that this particular snowfall had been the cause of considerable damage, and the workers in her household felt that they might be excused for their failure to control the snow if Mrs. Eddy were informed that the storm was almost country-wide and not confined to New England.

I had never seen Mr. Frye before, except as he occupied the seat beside the coachman, as Mrs. Eddy took her daily drive in Concord on the occasion of my last visit there. He was a short, stout man with pale and thoughtful countenance, indicating that he was accustomed to an indoor rather than an outdoor life. He was quiet, even to taciturnity, — extremely non-communicative, — and with an abruptness in his short answers that might have given the impression to a stranger that he was impatient with his questioner. I soon found, however, that this was not the case, but that at the time of my arrival he had been serving our Leader for a period of perhaps twenty-five years, and long association with her had taught him to mind his own business and he expected others to do the same. There was another side to Mr. Frye's character, also, and at times he was quite genial and friendly in his relations with the other members of the household. He possessed a keen sense of humor, and he was a man who liked his little joke quite as well as did others of a more mirthful disposition.

Mrs. Sargent I had met when she was the custodian of the room that had been furnished by the children for our Leader in The Mother Church. My wife and I visited this room in 1907, and it was Mrs. Sargent who showed us through the apartment. Her engaging manner and pleasant disposition made such a deep impression upon us then that we always thought of her as particularly amiable and loving. I found her devoted to Mrs. Eddy. She seemed to have but one thought and that was to serve, and the members of Mrs. Eddy's household who recall her, will always think of her as the loving and devoted Laura Sargent.

Another of the workers I had never met before, and I found her a wholesome, loving Christian Scientist who had been in our Leader's household for nearly a year. She remained but a short time after my arrival, returning to her home city where she had been long engaged as a teacher and practitioner. She will always be lovingly remembered by those who knew her best.

The student who was serving as secretary I already knew, having heard him read in one of the Churches of Christ, Scientist, in New York City. He was there temporarily filling the place of secretary, which had just been vacated by my predecessor, and I found that he was awaiting my arrival in order that he might return to his work in New York.

After breakfast this gentleman took me under his wing, as it were, and gave me a glimpse of the house as far as it was

11

practicable at that time. Many, who have visited Mrs. Eddy's home since her departure, will remember it as a large stone structure, massive in its lines. The front door opens from a *porte-cochere* into a vestibule, and thence into a large hall, which extends to the rear of the house, leading through French doors on to a balcony overlooking a wide expanse of territory, with the Blue Hills in the distance. On the right of the hall are two large rooms, the front one of which was used as the library, and the rear one as a dining room. Between these two rooms is a small transverse hall, leading out to the side door and the kitchen, which is crossed through large openings in which are hung heavy portieres. The windows in the dining room also look out over the rear of the estate toward the Blue Hills.

On the left of the front hall is an aperture, or little hall, about ten feet square in which stands the stately hall clock, surmounted by the Ambrose coat of arms of our Leader's mother's family. From this antechamber one enters the large drawing rooms extending from the front to the rear and giving an idea of space and expansion to the whole house. In these rooms tastefully displayed are many beautiful rugs, paintings, and other ornaments, which have been presented to our Leader from time to time by her devoted followers. The windows at the rear of these two rooms open, as do those of the dining room, on to the balcony referred to, and a large opening on the right enables one to pass through the spacious hall into the dining room, and in this way to make the complete circuit from room to room of the lower floor. The house was newly furnished and carpeted throughout, this arduous labor having been performed under the supervision of a member of The Mother Church who was selected for this particular work.

From the front of the hall on the right rises the large colonial staircase, easy of ascent and extending well back to the second floor with its old, high ceilings. After being shown the lower floor, I was taken to the room which was to be mine, directly over the library at the front of the house and on the same floor with the rooms occupied by our Leader. I found it equipped as an office, as well as a bedroom. There were house telephones connecting with every room in the house except those occupied by Mrs. Eddy. The room was large, light, airy, and well furnished. My guide soon seated himself with me at the desk and began to give me an outline of what my duties were to be. This was the first intimation I had had that there was a possibility that I might serve Mrs. Eddy in a secretarial capacity. There were numerous letters on the desk from various places, all of which had been opened by the secretary *pro tem*. He told me many interesting things regarding our Leader's daily routine, — the hour when she arose, when she breakfasted, when she received and read her mail, as well as many others of her daily tasks, which were performed at a set hour. I have always felt grateful for this friend. He was the first and only one, other than Mrs. Eddy herself, to give me any satisfactory explanation as to why I was there, and why others were there also. He gave me a short sketch of the people in the house and also gave me bits of information that proved valuable to me afterward.

Remaining for a little over two weeks, this student then returned to his home in New York, and shortly afterward his place was taken by another worker who came at our Leader's request and was accepted as a member of her household.

I was informed of Mr. Frye's association with Mrs. Eddy, and was told that he had been in her employ for about twenty-five years. Mr. Frye originally worked in one of the shoe shops of Lynn, Massachusetts, where he operated a machine of some description. He was a man of meager education, but through reading and observation had cultivated a high degree of understanding. He was religious and devout by nature, and was identified with a church in Lynn when he became interested in Christian Science. This occurred shortly after the passing on of his wife, and upon learning something of the teachings of Christian Science, he went through a class with Mrs. Eddy in the year 1881, and manifested a deep

13

interest in her work. His devotion to the Cause of Christian Science attracted the attention of our Leader, and being at the time without any secretarial help, she turned to Mr. Frye to perform many little services for her, which he did with such eagerness and thoroughness that she eventually employed him as a sort of *factotum*, and he finally became a member of her household. He assisted her in arranging and calling her classes; he tended the furnace, and in fact, did everything he could in the way of service to relieve our Leader from thought-taking or annoyances in connection with her great work. When she moved to Concord, New Hampshire, he went with her and always accompanied her on her daily drives, so that Calvin Frye came to be a household necessity with Mrs. Eddy. She told me that she found him scrupulously honest and trustworthy, and eventually she turned over to him the keeping of her accounts. He was her bookkeeper and cashier, as well as her secretary. At the time of my entry into Mrs. Eddy's household, Mr. Frye sat at the head of the table and was virtually the host, so that when my informant whispered to me, "If I were you, I would cultivate Frye," it spoke volumes, and showed me that because of his intense devotion and service to Mrs. Eddy, he was one of the most valued members of her household.

Chapter III

FIRST MEETING WITH MRS. EDDY

The morning mail had just arrived, and one of my first discoveries was that everything in the way of mail, packages, and things to be receipted for, came into the house via the secretary's office. I was almost startled to see the acting secretary pick up a letter opener and begin opening Mrs. Eddy's mail. He then explained that he was doing this under Mrs. Eddy's direction, and that if I were to continue as her secretary, she would give me similar instructions.

About this time a knock came at the door and Mr. Frye informed me that Mrs. Eddy wished to see me. I think my heart gave a few extra flutters, for this was to me the supreme moment in my Christian Science career. I arose and followed him. He led me along the upstairs hall from the front of the house, diagonally across to a large room at the left and rear which was occupied by Mrs. Eddy as a study. Mr. Frye entered this room and I followed him. Mrs. Eddy was seated in a large chair beside her desk and as we entered she rose and extended her hand in greeting. After introducing me, Mr. Frye left the room.

Mrs. Eddy motioned me to a chair, and we had our first conversation. She was a woman of rather below medium height, slender, and having the appearance of a person between eighty and ninety years of age. Her complexion was clear and her eyes were bright. She talked with a most beautifully modulated voice. At times, when she was saying some unusually impressive thing, it took on qualities deep and orotund. It seemed like one of the best trained voices I had ever heard. Her hair was gray and becomingly arranged, and one thing that impressed me deeply was the daintiness and neatness of her attire. She wore the well-known diamond cross at her throat and a large marquise ring, set with diamonds, that she seemed to think a great deal of. Her dress was of heavy silk and cut and made without regard to the modes and fashions of that day. She wore a ruching about her neck, which I afterward learned was replaced every morning. She seldom appeared in the same dress on successive days and seemed to have a complete and inexhaustive wardrobe. In short, I soon discovered that Mrs. Eddy was fond of dress, and that she believed in daintiness, neatness, and order in connection with all her wearing apparel. Her hands were small and her fingernails were well manicured, a task which she imposed upon herself every morning.

After I was seated she asked me many questions, among which were, what my age was, my birthplace, my schooling, and under what circumstances I had come into Christian Science. She asked who my teacher was, what my success had been in healing, and many other interrogatories, which bore no particular significance to me at that time, but which I afterward learned she felt were important. She seemed pleased to know that I had not come into Christian Science in search of health, and was also interested to hear that I was one of nine children, all of whom were still living, with the father and mother, who had attained to a healthy old age. She was impressed with the fact that we rarely if ever had need for a physician in our family and that the fear of sickness and disease had been almost unknown.

She then gave me a brief outline of some of the duties she would expect of me, and asked me if I would like to come and live in her household and become a member of it, and enter her service as a mental worker. I told her I would be most happy if she would employ me in any capacity whatever. After a few more words she excused me and I left her study.

Upon reaching my own room I sat down and was meditating on what had occurred when I heard the sharp ringing of a bell four times in quick succession. Presently, Mr. Frye appeared at my door and said, "Mr. Dickey, that is your signal to come to Mrs. Eddy's room. Whenever you hear four bells, it means for you to respond at once to her call." I immediately went to her and she again spoke to me, — this time a little more intimately, about her personal affairs. She explained that as the Leader of a great Movement, she had naturally acquired many enemies, and that she was having considerable to meet by way of aggressive mental suggestion, intended to injure or affect her physically. This seemed a very startling disclosure at that time, but nevertheless I accepted it. After receiving some directions as to how I should work for our Leader, I again returned to my room and pondered over the things she had said to me.

The followers of a great leader usually feel, as they have a right to, that they are well acquainted with and thoroughly understand the person whom they are following. This, however, was not true in the case of Mrs. Eddy. Very few people really knew her at all intimately, with the exception of perhaps two or three of those who spent a great deal of time with her, and even then she was often heard to say that those who had been with her the longest seemed to know her the least. It was generally believed among Mrs. Eddy's followers that she stood erect physically and mentally at all times and simply spoke the word to error and it would entirely disappear. There were occasions when she did rise to this height, but there were also times when she seemed to bend beneath the heavy load that mortal mind had placed upon her, and it was then that she really yearned for human aid and sympathy. She seemed to feel that she was more or less alone in her sphere of work and that those by whom she was surrounded did not really understand her or sympathize with her in the way in which she truly wished. Mrs. Eddy was not what might be called a worldly-wise woman, and yet whenever a question of any kind arose that required a decision from the standpoint of wisdom, she was always able to appeal to the divine Mind and get her answer.

I arrived at the residence in Chestnut Hill, Thursday morning, February 6, 1908. On Sunday, the 9th, the coachman, who lived in a small cottage at some distance from the house, had not made his appearance, and someone whose duties took him to the barn brought the information to Mr. Frye that the horses had not been cared for that morning. An investigation was started, and it was nearly noon before it was discovered that the coachman had passed on some time during the night with a claim of heart failure, and when found *rigor mortis* had already set in.

This seemed to be one of the cases where there was so much anxiety on the part of the worker to obtain employment with Mrs. Eddy, that the unfortunate man informed the committee that he was in excellent health and had always been sound and well, although he had in times past been subject to attacks of this sort. He evidently did not realize that entering the employ of Mrs. Eddy would subject him to more vigorous attacks in this direction than he had ever sustained before. The discovery was made apparently too late to render the man assistance. In one short week he furnished an illustration of how quickly error would strike at those who undertook to render a service to our Leader.

After dinner, Mr. Frye came into my room and said that Mrs. Eddy was greatly disappointed in not being able to take her drive. "Why can't she take her drive?" I asked. "There is nobody to drive her." "Can't you?" I questioned. "No," he replied, "I never have driven a horse attached to a sleigh, and Mother is not willing for me to undertake it." "Would she like me to drive?" "Can you do it?" asked Mr. Frye. "Yes," I said, "I have been accustomed to horses all my life." When he informed Mrs. Eddy, she sent for me at once and questioned me about my ability to drive horses. I assured her that I was quite capable of performing this service for her and would be overjoyed to do it. This was my first experience in acting as coachman for Mrs. Eddy, but I was inwardly pleased to know that such a slight service meant so much to her.

In commenting upon the passing on of her coachman she opened *Science and Health*, and turned to page 187, line 13, and at the same time she said to me, "Mr. Dickey, when I turn to this book, I am like a mechanic who turns to his tools and picks up the one he wants. This reference on page 187 has a direct bearing on the case. When it occurred I knew where it came from, for it presented itself clearly to me in thought." After a short discussion of the subtle claims of malicious mental malpractice, she dictated what now appears in *Science and Health* (page 442, line 30-32).

I drove the sleigh each day until a new coachman was installed, which was on Thursday, February 13.

It was Mrs. Eddy's custom to arise promptly at six o'clock every morning. She rang the bell for her maid at that hour and one touch of the bell always called her. One could almost set his watch by the regularity with which this bell was rung. Mrs. Eddy did not breakfast with the family. Her meals were taken in her own apartment, and her light breakfast was served by her maid at seven o'clock, which was also the hour for the family breakfast.

The system of bells in Mrs. Eddy's house was a great institution. I think it must have been improvised by Mr. Frye, and at first thought, one would be inclined to believe that a much better device might have been arranged. On longer acquaintance, however, it was found that this crude system of bell ringing was about the only one that could be effectively put into operation. A single cord with a button was located at a convenient place on Mrs. Eddy's desk and the bells were connected in series, that is to say, when one touch was given to the button, one bell rang in the maid's room, in the upper hall, in the lower hall, and in the kitchen. This was done so that in whatever part of the house the maid may have been at the time the bell was rung, it would not escape her attention. Each worker had a definite ring, three, four, or five, or whatever the number might be, and if any worker left the home, his successor inherited the same number of bells. When Mrs. Eddy desired

19

to call all of her workers together at one time, she usually gave the bell ten or fifteen taps, which always resulted in the quick appearance of her mental workers.

The first morning I experienced this wholesale calling was a few days after my arrival, when I heard the bells ringing apparently all over the house. I was still wondering what the commotion was about when Mr. Frye shoved his head through my door and said, "That means everybody." I responded with alacrity and found that others had arrived before me because of my ignorance as to what this sudden call meant.

Mrs. Eddy opened the Bible and read to us James 1, verses 21-25. Then she gave us all a talk on being "doers of the word, and not hearers only," deceiving ourselves. She dwelt especially on the passage referring to a man beholding his natural face in a glass and straightway forgetting what manner of man he was. This brought out a new meaning to me that affected the whole passage, and I saw the right idea of man as never before. Our difficulty seems to be that we look at the reflection mortal mind sends back and accept this as our true being, forgetting that man is spiritual and not material. She said to us, "You are not doing your work as you should and I shall not instruct you further until you have demonstrated something more of what has been taught. It would be a poor teacher that would take students up into the higher branches of mathematics before they had proved addition, subtraction, multiplication, and division. Therefore, until you demonstrate in better fashion what you have already been taught, I shall teach you no more." This is one of the gentle means of persuasion our Leader so often employed in endeavoring to get us to do better work. The reader here should understand that the people employed in Mrs. Eddy's home were there for but one purpose, and that was to serve their Leader and to protect her against malicious attacks of mortal mind in her endeavors to give to the world the religion of Christian Science. At this point I can almost hear some critical reader say,

20

"What nonsense! Who is trying maliciously to attack Mrs. Eddy?" Remember the people's reply to Jesus, "Thou hast a devil: who goeth about to kill thee?" (John 7:20.) Many times she struggled with some physical argument that had to be met before she could proceed with her regular work of directing the Movement. Not only was it incumbent on her to keep a clear thought of the demands made upon her in her direction and control of The Mother Church and its branches, but she also had to keep her head above the malicious and intentionally directed attacks made upon her personally, having for their purpose and sole object the interruption of her work and the attempt, if possible, to destroy her life.

On the following morning she spoke to me about the determination we should exercise in doing our mental work. She said, "Never fear a lie. Declare against it with the consciousness of its nothingness. Throw your whole weight into the right scale. This is the only way to destroy evil." She then picked up a lead pencil from her desk, and grasping it in the middle with her thumb and forefinger, she balanced it there like a pair of scales. Then she touched the point with one of her fingers and pressed it down, forcing the other end of the pencil up, and said, "You can see that whatever you put in one end of the scale always throws the other end up. Now remember this, and never admit anything that will weigh against ourselves. When we admit a lie, we put the weight into the wrong scale, and this operates against ourselves."

Chapter IV

"GENERAL QUARTERS" AT HOME

I was beginning now to become better acquainted with my duties and with what was expected of Mrs. Eddy's workers at Chestnut Hill. The household consisted at this time of about twelve members besides Mrs. Eddy. Included among the twelve were two gentlemen and two ladies; Mrs. Eddy's personal maid; another, who, with her own hands, prepared our Leader's meals; the house man, who was Mrs. Eddy's trusted servant; the night watchman; the housekeeper; and the coachman who took care of the stables. All of these dear people had left their homes and had come as associate workers in our Leader's house to serve her and the Cause of Christian Science.

Occasionally changes took place in the personnel of the household, it becoming necessary for one cause or another to bring in new workers, and allow the older ones to return to their homes. At times the number of those present went as high as sixteen or eighteen, so that there was quite a house full of people.

The main object in the thought of everyone was to do what he could to serve Mrs. Eddy. She was endeavoring to live and carry on the work which God had given her to do, and when things went well with her, there was a spirit of cheerfulness and activity throughout the household that seemed to be reflected in the conduct of each individual member; but when Mrs. Eddy seemed to be laboring under the oft-repeated attacks of evil, the members of her household kept busily at work.

The most important work in connection with our Leader's home was that done by the mental workers, who were there because of their experience in the field as practitioners and of their ability to handle the claims of evil as they presented themselves. This work was done under the direct supervision of our Leader, and through her secretary she informed the other workers just what phases of error she felt should be given special attention. Her secretary, at her request, prepared what was denominated a "watch." This consisted of typewritten sheets of paper containing in numerical order the names or description of the phases of error that Mrs. Eddy wished them to handle. She was being constantly assailed by mental malpractice, and it was necessary for someone to take up this work and aid her in freeing herself from these different attacks. She seemed to be the only one who was able to discern the course that error was pursuing. Sometimes she learned this through suffering, but she always knew it and would by means of these "watches" notify the workers what their mental work should be. Many times, while our Leader was working on the problems connected with the government of her Church, the physical effects of the discord she wished to overcome seemed to manifest themselves in her body, and often she was prostrated with suffering, apparently caused by the chemicalization of the conditions of thought she was endeavoring to meet, and which seemed to culminate in her own thought.

Some of the most important By-laws of The Mother Church formulated themselves in the thought of our Leader while she was under a claim of suffering, which continued until the By-law was ready to be passed upon by the Directors. Then the suffering disappeared and everything went on harmoniously without a single trace of what our Leader had passed through.

These experiences occurred when she changed the By-laws, doing away with the Communion Service in The Mother Church, and also on the occasion when she disbanded the executive members of The Mother Church. She suffered greatly in both these instances, but the moment she arrived at a decision and framed the By-laws which treated with these two conditions, her relief was instantaneous and she arose immediately, healed. This caused me to ponder much, and recall the quotation from Isaiah (53:4-5) where he says: "Surely he hath borne our griefs, and carried our sorrows: yet we did esteem him stricken, smitten of God, and afflicted. But he was wounded for our transgressions, he was bruised for our iniquities: the chastisement of our peace was upon him; and with his stripes we are healed."

Calvin Frye told me that these experiences always came to Mrs. Eddy in this way and that whenever any great revelation came to her, concerning that which seemed necessary for the welfare of our Cause, these struggles appeared in her body. This corroborates what she told me about feeling the needs of the Movement in her body.

On one of these occasions, when her suffering seemed severe, she called us all into the room and quoted a passage from Shakespeare's *Macbeth*:

Canst thou not minister to a mind diseas'd,
Pluck from the memory a rooted sorrow,
Raze out the written troubles of the brain,
And with some sweet oblivious antidote
Cleanse the stuff'd bosom of that perilous stuff
Which weighs upon the heart?

It was at this time that she said to us, "You don't any of you realize what is going on. This is a dark hour for the Cause and you do not seem to be awake to it." She said, "I am now working on a plane that would mean instantaneous death to any of you."

Each mental worker in the home occupied his own room, which was large, airy, and comfortably furnished, with private bath connected. The injunction, "Never forsake your post," was one that was strictly obeyed by every mental worker in our Leader's home. Each was always to be found in his own room, and when a change was proposed in the line of mental work to be taken up, Mrs. Eddy would give her secretary the language of the "watch," or perhaps it would be sent to his room by Mr. Frye, Mrs. Sargent, or Mrs. Eddy's maid, whichever one happened to be convenient when the inspiration reached our Leader. Carbon copies were made of these "watches" and one was taken directly to the room of each worker, as a guide to him in his mental work. The subjects covered by these "watches" were endless in their variety. One thing in particular that our Leader requested her workers to care for was the weather, and this was done in addition to the work of the committee in Boston appointed for that special purpose. During some of the severe New England winters when a greater amount of snow than usual was falling, our Leader would instruct her workers that they must put a stop to what seemed to be the steadily increasing fall of snow which she looked upon as a manifestation of error. She had an aversion to an excessive fall of snow. She considered it as an agent of destruction, an interference with the natural and normal trend of business. We are quick to recognize the fact that an unusually heavy fall of snow in any community is a disastrous thing. It clogs the wheels of commerce, interferes with traffic, interrupts the regular routine of business affairs, and breaks in upon the harmony and continuity of man's peaceful existence. Millions of dollars are spent annually in many places to remove the effects of heavy snowfalls, and so this was one of the points that was covered by Mrs. Eddy's mental workers. One of the "watches" issued January 15, 1910, requested her mental workers to "Make a law that there shall be no more snow this season."

When our Leader first came to live at Chestnut Hill in the spring and summer of 1908, thunder storms and electric disturbances seemed to be unusually prevalent. This was another form of error which our Leader disliked very much. A gentle rainfall was a delight to her, but a destructive, electrical storm she abhorred. She evidently looked upon it as a manifestation of evil and a destructive agency of mortal mind. Mrs. Sargent was the one to whom was especially assigned the work of watching the weather and bringing it into accord with normal conditions. For the three years during our Leaders's stay in Chestnut Hill, and for several years thereafter, the recollection of the writer is that there were fewer and fewer thunder storms until they almost ceased to be.

Upon one occasion after she had given her workers some instructions regarding the weather, and after we had all repaired to our several rooms to continue, a succession of taps on her bell called us all back into her sitting room, where, as was our custom, we arranged ourselves in front of her chair very much as the old-fashioned class in school arranged itself in front of the schoolmaster. Pointing with her finger to the first one in the class, which happened to be myself, she said, "Mr. Dickey, can a Christian Scientist control the weather?" "Yes, Mother." To the next person, "Can a Christian Scientist control the weather?" "Yes, Mother." To the next, "Can a Christian Scientist control the weather?" "Yes, Mother." "Mr. Frye, can a Christian Scientist control the weather?" "Yes, Mother." To the next person, "Can a Christian Scientist control the weather?" "Yes, Mother." This question was put to each member of the class with the same reply. After we had all repeated our answers, an expression of rejection, not to say scorn, came upon her face, and she said with emphasis, "They can't and they don't." This brought a look of surprise to the face of each member of the class, for we had just been instructed, as we thought, how to take care of the weather. She repeated the statement, "They can't," but immediately she added, "but God can and does. Now," she said, "I want you to see the point I am making. A Christian Scientist has no business attempting to control or govern the weather any more than he has a right to attempt to control or govern sickness, but he does know, and must know, that God governs the weather and no other influence can be brought to bear upon it. When we destroy mortal mind's belief that it is a creator, and that it produces all sorts of weather, good as well as bad, we shall then realize God's perfect weather and be the recipients of His bounty in that respect. God's weather is always right. A certain amount of rain and sunshine is natural and normal, and we have no right to interfere with the stately operations of divine Wisdom in regulating meteorological conditions. Now I called you back because I felt you did not get my former instructions correctly and I want you to remember that the weather belongs to God, and when we destroy the operations of mortal mind and leave the question of regulating the weather to God, we shall have weather conditions as they should be."

Every Christian Scientist will see the force of our Leader's instruction in this respect. Mortal mind's attempts to take out of the hands of the Creator of the universe His dispensation of weather should be met and overcome through the realization of what really constitutes God's government regarding the weather.

I have heard our Leader describe in a number of instances how she has dissipated a thunder cloud by simply looking upon it and bringing to bear upon mortal mind's concept of this manifestation of discord what God really has prepared for us, and she illustrated this by a wave of her hand indicating the total disappearance of the thunder cloud and its accompanying threat.

As time went on, the serious nature of our work at Chestnut Hill dawned upon my thought. I saw that we were there filling one of the most important positions that could be assigned to human kind.

The Leader and Founder of a great Movement was casting her thought over the welfare of the whole world. Christian Science, if it means anything, is designed to save the world from the penalities of its own sins and shortcomings, as exhibited in sickness, sin, and death. Its purpose is to destroy and annihilate the claims of evil of every sort. Then it is not surprising that evil, which

27

has a belief of intelligence, would retaliate by training its guns on the citadel of Christian Science and attempt to destroy that which is surely and effectually ridding the world of evil and all kindred beliefs. To have an assignment, then, as a protector and bodyguard of the Leader of this Movement, and be permitted to share in the defence of its Discoverer and Founder, is an assignment of no small moment. Many times our Leader was attacked through mental influences of the most sinister and wicked nature.

In olden times the occupants of a fortress were attacked from without by means of bombardment of missiles of all sorts. There were intrigue, treachery, conspiracies, and plans brought into execution that had for their object the downfall of the citadel which was being attacked. The commandant of the fortress was aware of these methods of attack, and it was no difficult thing to provide against the onslaught of the enemy by reinforcing the battered walls and throwing up a shield of defense against the visible material missiles that were hurled against them, but in these days of cultivated thought, when the power of a mental assault is recognized, when mortal mind has changed its basis of attack from material missiles to mental shafts, they cannot be turned back by material walls. The defence of the headquarters of the Christian Science Movement must be conducted in a vastly different way from that of the old-fashioned fortress. The educated and liberated mortal thought of today is employing its weapons of mental warfare surely and effectually as it did the more grossly material weapons of former years, unless the Christian Scientist builds a strong defence. From the time Mrs. Eddy first began to preach and teach Christian Science, every conceivable form of weapon was turned against her in the hope that her work could be stopped and that evil would be left to its own devices in its attempts to control mankind.

When the stones were first hurled through the windows of her lecture room and onto the platform where she stood, she realized that she was fighting an uphill fight and that she had enlisted in a warfare, the purpose of which was the destruction of the highest forms of evil. In the later years of her Leadership there was no cessation or even diminution of these mental attacks upon her, but they continued with ever-increasing volume in the attempt to destroy her life and obliterate her work. It was for this reason that Mrs. Eddy called effectual workers around her. For this reason also they were sought out, examined, and questioned in regard to their ability to prove the teachings of Christian Science, and then brought to Chestnut Hill to form a body-guard or a defence for our Leader in the continuation of her work.

Chapter V

THE IDEAL OF ORDERLINESS
AND REGULARITY

Mrs. Eddy had lived for so long in her comparatively small home in Concord, New Hampshire, that the transition from this rather diminutive residence to the large, commodious home in Chestnut Hill introduced a sudden change in her daily routine that at times made it a bit awkward for her. It is true that the plan of the house at Chestnut Hill bore a striking resemblance to the one she had just vacated in Concord so far as the location of the rooms was concerned, but everything seemed so gigantic and extensive to our Leader that these circumstances troubled her not a little. She, therefore, decided to have some alterations made, and an architect from the west was sent for to effect the needed changes.

Her study at Concord was a room perhaps fourteen by sixteen feet, while the corresponding room in her Chestnut Hill house, which was used by her as a study, was at least twenty feet by twenty. Mrs. Eddy's desk and chair were located in the circular bay window and the door, by means of which workers entered the room, was in the corner diagonally opposite. In complaining about the size of the rooms, our Leader humorously said that when she called a student to come to her, she could not wait while he walked across such a great expanse of carpet from the door to where she sat, and something must be done to conserve her time. It was too valuable to waste in waiting for people to walk across a large room. Happily, through the architect's skill the changes were easily designed, and Mrs. Eddy moved her suite to the third floor, while the necessary alterations were being made in her own apartment. The changes consisted in reducing the size of her study, in cutting down the dimensions of her bedroom, and in taking enough from the latter and adding it to Mr. Frye's room so that he might have a bedroom and a sitting room instead of one large room.

Orderliness, neatness, and dispatch were among the leading characteristics of our Leader, and to discommode herself, by moving to the third floor, where the ceilings and the walls of the room conformed to the slant of the roof, meant no little change in her environment. Here she lived for nearly three weeks, while the workmen labored night and day to make the needed changes on the floor below. A large staircase was constructed leading from the second to the third floor, space for which was taken out of her study. Partitions had to be removed and others erected. Gas pipes and electric conduits had to be cut and changed; the floors had to be somewhat torn up in places, and an electric elevator installed from a small entry leading from her study to the *porte-cochere* below, at the side entrance of the house, from which our Leader took her daily drive.

The carpenters, plumbers, gasfitters, electricians, painters, paper hangers, and iron workers all did their work smoothly and well, so that the whole change was effected expeditiously and with a degree of harmony that is seldom seen in alteration work of this character. The move back to her own rooms on the second floor was accomplished with little difficulty, every member of the household lending a willing hand. The pictures had to be rehung, the ornaments on the mantel and elsewhere in the room had to be placed in their proper positions, and with this I learned something about the character of our Leader, which was most interesting and helpful to me.

I had always heard that it was difficult for her to find people who would carry out her orders implicitly, and when I entered her employ, one of the obligations I placed upon myself was to obey her absolutely, without question, no matter what she might ask me to do. It did not take Mrs. Eddy long to discover this quality of obedience in my thought, and she at once evidenced a pleasure in having me do things for her, so that when she moved into her new room and settled it, I was privileged to stand at her hand and place everything where she wished it. She herself named the spot on the mantel where each ornament should rest, while I, overjoyed at this rare privilege, moved things back and forth at her command until everything was placed as she desired it. She superintended the hanging of all the pictures in her house, but was more careful of those hung in her bedroom, study, and sitting room. They, too, were changed many times until she had them just where she wanted them. The ornaments on her bookcase and chiffonier were also changed about until they suited her, indicating to me that she looked upon each object as an expression of thought, and she wanted that thought to harmonize with the mental atmosphere of her room.

Sometimes a thoughtless assistant in cleaning or tidying her room would leave something out of place, and Mrs. Eddy, upon her return, would immediately notice the disarrangement, asking why things were not as she had left them. She seemed to feel that a room was out of balance mentally. Occasionally the one who was responsible for this displacement would insist that everything had been returned exactly as it was before the room was disturbed. This resulted in two annoying situations. In the one instance our Leader felt that her assistant had not the right mental attitude toward her, while on the other hand the assistant felt that Mrs. Eddy was unnecessarily exacting, or that it was a caprice on her part, and that she was not always right in her criticisms. Never have I found our Leader to be wrong, however, in a case of this kind.

By reason of my close association with her, there grew up an intimacy between our Leader's thought and my own that furnished me opportunities for observation and acquaintance with her methods and caused me to see that she was always right whenever a difference of opinion existed between her and any of her followers.

It was the custom of the workers in the house, when it became necessary to sweep and dust Mrs. Eddy's rooms, to perform this service while she was out on her daily drive, so that when she returned all evidences of the cleaning operation would be removed. The workers soon found by experience that it would not do to replace anything that had to be moved in a disorderly or slovenly manner. Experience taught them that unless everything was returned to its proper place, there would be a reprimand forthcoming from our Leader, and this occurred so frequently that the attendants were troubled in their efforts to get everything back exactly as they found it. In order, then, that no mistakes should be made and that they might not yield to the argument of error that they could not please Mrs. Eddy, a tiny brass tack was driven into the floor through the carpet, marking the place where each piece of furniture belonged, and always when she returned she would find everything just as she had left it. When once this habit of orderliness was formed by the houseworkers, they found their tasks lighter and everything made easier by reason of the fact that the furniture could be quickly put back in its rightful place and no time be consumed in guessing or wondering if things looked just right. They also discovered that Mrs. Eddy was always right in her complaints about the misplaced furniture, for after they adopted the placing of brass tacks, no more objections came from her.

If our Leader had not insisted that everything should occupy its proper place, one can easily see how error would so have handled the workers that her room would never have been orderly, or arranged twice in the same way. This may seem like a small matter for Mrs. Eddy to complain of, but when we study the situation and see that her room represented to her a condition of thought, it at once becomes explicable. To her every picture, every ornament, and piece of furniture in her rooms represented a thought, and when these were rightly adjusted, her thought was undisturbed, but to disturb the furniture would be to disturb her thought, and this is why she insisted that everything must be properly arranged and duly adjusted. This illustrated the fact that, even in such a simple thing as sweeping a room and rearranging the furniture, the following of a definite rule of Principle makes everything easier.

Orderliness and promptness grew to be a habit with the members of Mrs. Eddy's household. There was a clock in every room. Each member of the household had his own timepiece, and it was expected to be always in perfect running order. In Mrs. Eddy's sitting room there were three clocks. In her bedroom there were two, one of which was an old-fashioned alarm clock which she had fastened to the foot of her bed. This was done so that in the night, by simply turning on the light, she would know instantly what hour it was. On a table beside her bed she kept a tablet of paper and a pencil, and many times thoughts that came to her in the night were written down for preservation. This obviated the necessity of her doing what she did when the title of her Textbook, *Science and Health*, came to her. (*Message for 1902*, page 15, line 25.)

Breakfast for the household was served promptly at seven o'clock every morning, and no one needed to be called or sent for. No announcement was made that breakfast was served. The fact is that at seven o'clock the members of the household walked into the dining room, and promptly at seven o'clock the associate worker placed the breakfast on the table. At noon the same general order prevailed, and everyone presented himself promptly in the dining room at twelve o'clock. No gong was sounded, no dinner bell, no summons of anyone. They were all there at the right time. This was also the case in the evening, so that everything at Chestnut Hill moved with the promptness and regularity of clockwork. There was no confusion, no friction, no lost time. Indeed, the question of meals and mealtime occupied very little space in the thought of the members of Mrs. Eddy's household. They grew into the habit of being in their place at the proper time. No matter what the obligation or duty was which had to be performed, if it could be arranged so as to be done in regular order, it was so arranged, and in this way tasks were lightened and duties were made a pleasure by having a regular hour at which to perform everything.

Notwithstanding the fact that our Leader's time was greatly taken up with the most exacting and arduous labors for her Cause, she nevertheless seemed to have ample time to devote to the appearance of her house, both inside and out. She noticed that one of the trees on her place did not appear to thrive, but was drooping and showing every evidence of dying. She learned that the superintendent of her grounds proposed to cut the tree down and remove it. Immediately she sent word to him to do nothing of the kind, but to do what he could for the tree in his way, while she took the question up according to Christian Science. In a remarkably short time the tree began to grow and thrive, and today it occupies a place on her grounds.

Her driveway claimed a share of her attention, and at one time she stopped the workmen from constructing a cement gutter from the gate to the house. Afterward I was obliged to inform her that three of the trustees, in whose hands she had placed the management of her entire estate, had approved and accepted the contract made by her superintendent for the construction of the cement gutter in question. It seems that the trustees had been informed that Mrs. Eddy had given her consent to the installation of the gutter, which was a mistake. Hence, the objection that came from our Leader. A note in her own handwriting reads, "Obtain for me the legal consent of the Directors to defer the job on this side of the driveway 'til I say in writing I am ready for it." There was something about this particular piece of work that was objectionable to Mrs. Eddy and her thought rebelled against it.

35

On another occasion, when Mrs. Eddy noticed that the iron work on exposed parts of her house needed painting, she called me to her and said, "This iron work should be painted in order that it may be properly protected from rust, which is so prevalent near salt air." Whereupon she dictated the following letter to Mr. Archibald McLellan:

> *Beloved Student:*
> *Send me a painter to simply paint some iron outside. I want him just as soon as you can get him.*
> *Lovingly yours,*
> *MARY BAKER EDDY.*

One would think that the leader of a great movement would have little time to spare for such material incidentals as the foregoing, but Mrs. Eddy's active thought seemed to take in everything that was necessary for the protection of her home, and incidents of this nature were of more or less frequent occurrence.

Mrs. Eddy never let down on anything. She kept everything up to the highest point of perfection, — her appearance, her hair, her finger-nails, her house, her horses and carriage, — in fact, none of the evidences of age or neglect were ever allowed to show themselves. She admired pretty things and beautiful things as one may infer from a letter to the St. Louis church, in which she points out that it is not evil to enjoy good things but that it is evil to be a slave to pleasure. (*The First Church of Christ, Scientist, and Miscellany*, page 197, lines 1-2.) A short while before she left us she ordered a new carriage, while the old one seemed to me in perfectly good condition. She seemed to realize thoroughly that things are thoughts, and that the most beautiful things express the clearest and most advanced thought. It was a law with Mrs. Eddy that everything had its rightful place and must always be in that place.

36

Upon answering my bell one day, I found our Leader in her parlor adjoining the study, sitting facing an old-fashioned whatnot. "Mr. Dickey," she said when I approached her, "I have been thinking of this whatnot. It seems so childish, and I believe I had better part with it. What do you think about it?" I saw that she was fond of this quaint bit of furniture and replied reassuringly, "Mother, everything on that whatnot represents someone's love and appreciation for you, and there is no reason why you should not have it." This seemed to satisfy her, and after a pause, she said, "Mr. Dickey, you always say the right thing. I'll keep it." And it stands today just as she left it.

After her removal from Concord to Chestnut Hill, our Leader set the time of taking her daily drive at one o'clock. At this hour her carriage always drove to the side entrance, where she was accustomed to enter the vehicle. One thing was not definitely set, and this was the duration of her drive. She seldom remained out longer than half an hour and returned as the demands upon her time appealed to her. It was a long drive from her home to The Mother Church, and only once during her residence at Chestnut Hill did she take the time to drive to Falmouth and St. Paul Streets, and then she did not alight, but had her first view of The Mother Church [Extension] from her carriage.

A daily drive with Mrs. Eddy was not a pleasure, nor in any sense a recreation. She did it because she felt obligated to do so in order to refute the constant charges that she was dead or incapacitated. She knew that as long as she appeared in her carriage every day, it would satisfy mortal mind and meet the charge that she had already departed and was no longer with us. There were times when it was a very severe task to take this drive. Indeed, as time went on, this obligation grew more irksome to her, and on many occasions she drove when she did not seem physically able to do so, but she did it nevertheless and always succeeded in meeting the attacks upon her so that she returned master of the situation.

On one occasion, just prior to her leaving the house for her drive, my bell rang and I responded immediately to find her seated in a chair dressed for her drive, painfully drawing on her gloves. She said to me, "Mr. Dickey, I want you to know that it does me good to go on this drive." Instantly she felt my questioning thought and she replied, "I do not mean that the physical going for a drive does me good, but the enemy have made a law that it hurts me to go on this drive, and they are trying to enforce it, while I want you to take the opposite stand with God and know that every act I perform in His service does me good. I do not take this drive for recreation, but because I want to establish my dominion over mortal mind's antagonistic beliefs." I at once saw the point she was making and replied to her with encouraging statements of Truth from her own book, and in a few moments every trace of the attack had disappeared, and she was herself again, ready to take her departure. Before doing so, however, she said, "Mr. Dickey, I want you to see what we have done. We have routed the enemy and broken the belief that it injured me to go on this drive. Now take this lesson to yourself, and whenever anything happens to you of an unfortunate nature, do not admit anything on the wrong side, but instantly declare that the experience does you good. Even if you should fall down and break your leg, get up and say, 'I am better for this experience.' This is the Truth as God would declare it, for every attempt of evil, when surmounted and destroyed, helps the one who is attacked, and your quick and right declaration to the effect that instead of harming you, it has done you good, breaks the claim of evil, and you become a law to yourself that evil cannot harm you."

Chapter VI

GENEROSITY — A LIFELONG CHARACTERISTIC

A more generous person than Mrs. Eddy, I never knew. She endeavored in every way to love her enemies and do good to those who sought to injure her. This was made evident on one occasion when it was brought to Mrs. Eddy's attention that a neighboring woman, through a belief of curiosity, was training a pair of field glasses on Mrs. Eddy's windows in the hope that she might see something that would interest her. She was also making it a practice to watch for our Leader when she took her daily drive with the anticipation of obtaining a view of her. Without discussing the question at all, or exhibiting the least evidence of annoyance, Mrs. Eddy sent this prying neighbor a basket of beautiful fruit, and when the coachman delivered it and told the woman that it was from Mrs. Eddy, she said, "Did that dear old lady send this fruit to me?" He replied, "Yes," and with a tearful voice the woman said, "Won't you give her my love and tell her I do appreciate this gift and thank her most kindly for it?" From this time on no attempt was made from that quarter to intrude upon Mrs. Eddy's privacy.

Our Leader loved to share what she had with others. When people sent her beautiful flowers, it was a rare thing for them to remain on her desk very long, and after she had admired and enjoyed them for a few moments, she would always thank the donor and pass them along to someone else. She would frequently send them to the rooms of some of the workers in the house or to the home of neighboring Christian Scientists whom she knew. Her thought seemed to be that in passing these gifts along, she was making them do double service and distributing the love and joy that their presence brought.

To the students who were close to her, she frequently made gifts of money, or some valuable article of jewelry, rings, pins, and so on. It just seemed to be her nature to want to give and it was an inclination that she did not attempt to curb. Many times her monetary gifts were quite substantial. This characteristic of giving was one which followed Mrs. Eddy from early years. She told me that when she was a child she used to give away her playthings to poor children, and sometimes even her dresses, until her mother had to threaten her saying that she would have to punish her if she did not stop giving away her belongings.

When the little book of poems, in the white and gold with the wild rose design, first appeared, it was privately printed by our Leader, and the copies were sent to Chestnut Hill. These were received as usual at the secretary's office, and I immediately carried in one of the books for our Leader to see. At once she asked me to read something from it. I opened to the poem called "Constancy," and read this. When I had finished reading, I looked up and saw that tears were streaming down her cheeks. "Mr. Dickey," she said feelingly, "that was written after I lost my husband." Then she autographed the first copy, numbering it "1," and gave it to me.

Not only in little things, but in more important directions Mrs. Eddy showed her generosity. She was a constant contributor, through Mr. Frye, to various charitable institutions, and the callers at her home asking for such contributions were very numerous. Sometimes her generosity was imposed upon. Shortly after her arrival in Chestnut Hill, at a friend's request, she gave her check for five hundred dollars as a contribution toward the Newton City Hospital. This was done in the spirit of good citizenship, since she remarked as she handed me the check, "I don't know why I am doing this, but I presume it is to please my friends."

GENEROUSITY — A LIFE-LONG CHARACTERISTIC

At one time Mrs. Eddy received an invitation from the pro-
moters of the Lincoln Memorial at Washington to join as a founder.
The invitation solicited a subscription to the cost of the Memorial,
and stated that contributions were being made by the most prominent citizens of our country. It was beautifully engraved, and when
I took it to Mrs. Eddy she asked me what I thought about it all. I
said, "Mother, I think people should be constructing a memorial to
you and your work instead of your contributing to anything of this
kind for somebody else." "Yes, Mr. Dickey," she replied, "but these
things are needed in the world today and it is natural for the citizens
of the United States to recognize the greatness and grandeur of
Abraham Lincoln's character. I shall send them a check for one
hundred dollars." And she did so. That is the way she followed my
advice.

Chapter VII

"WIT, HUMOR, AND ENDURING VIVACITY"
ACCURACY IN THOUGHT AND DEED

From what has previously been said, the reader must not think that there was never anything but work of a strenuous kind at Chestnut Hill. There were days, and even weeks, when the clouds seemed to lift and the workers in the home had time for self-advancement, and even for some little recreation. Mrs. Eddy was naturally of a bright and vivacious disposition. She had a wonderfully keen sense of humor, and never failed to see that side of an incident. Even while she was stimulating and admonishing her workers to better efforts, sometimes the serious look on their faces would bring forth a smile on her part. Even in the midst of the most serious admonition she would with difficulty restrain a smile, and I could see by the twitching of her lips that she saw the funny side of the situation and was amused within herself at the protestations and promises of better work on the part of her students. On one occasion when we all protested that we would do better, she smiled and said, "I am afraid you are like the Irishman that used to work on my father's farm. He was so useless about the place that my father finally called him and said, 'Mike, I shall have to let you go. You're not earning what I am paying you and it is not right for me to keep you under the circumstances.' Rather than be discharged, the Irishman pleaded to be kept in my father's employ. He said, 'If you'll only keep me, sir, I will work for my week's board.' 'But,' replied Mr. Baker, 'you don't earn your board in a week.' 'Well, sir,' he said, 'if I can't earn it in one week, I'll do it in two.'" Our

Leader continued, "That is what your promises sound like to me. You are not doing your work as you should, and you protest that if you haven't done it heretofore, you will hereafter."

To illustrate the grasping nature of mortal mind, Mrs. Eddy told us upon another occasion of a neighbor who wanted to sell her father a horse. He was also an Irishman and represented the horse as perfectly sound, gentle in disposition, and having all the qualities of a family carriage horse. "My father said, 'I am afraid he is too skittish for me. My family needs a quiet animal that would not be frightened at anything.' 'Oh,' replied the neighbor, 'Mr. Baker, you couldn't scare this horse, no matter what you did.' My father replied, 'Why, that horse would jump if you were to say 'boo' at him.' The man stoutly denied this and offered to put the case to a test. It was arranged that Mr. Baker should crouch behind a large stump in the field and the owner was to ride the horse by the stump, when Mr. Baker would jump out and shout 'boo.' The arrangements were made, and the horse loped down by the stump, whereupon Mr. Baker jumped out, and throwing his arms in the air, yelled a vigorous 'boo.' The horse made a sudden lunge, and throwing his rider, dashed off across the country. The Irishman got up and brushing the dirt from his clothes said, 'Well, Mr. Baker, that was too big a 'boo' for such a small horse.'"

One of the chief characteristics displayed by Mrs. Eddy was her accuracy in everything she undertook to do. She left nothing unfinished or uncertain, but carried everything out with most painstaking exactness. She was unusually careful in her choice of words and would many times hold a letter for hours, refusing to allow it to go out until she had found the exact word to express her meaning. Sometimes two or three different dictionaries would be consulted, and then after the letter had been changed several times, she would recall it and make still another change. On these occasions, which were numerous, she would apologize to her secretary and say, "Mr. Dickey, won't you forgive me if I ask you to bring that letter to me again?" I always assured her that I was perfectly delighted to make every change she suggested, for I always saw the improvement in what she was giving out. It was no task for me to write a letter for her, and the mere circumstance of coming into her room in response to her bell was always a joy to me. Frequently she would quote that well-known phrase attributed to Michelangelo, "Trifles make perfection, but perfection is no trifle."

Shortly after the completion of The Mother Church Extension, the Directors obtained Mrs. Eddy's permission to place a marble statue of a woman kneeling in an attitude of prayer on a pedestal above the organ in The Mother Church [Extension]. When the statue was completed, the Directors wrote Mrs. Eddy to that effect, stating that they would like to have her final permission to have the statue placed in position. In reply to this letter she wrote declining to give her consent. When it was explained to her that the statue had been ordered with her permission, and that the Directors felt under obligation to take it, this brought forth from her a very decisive letter which ended the incident, and the statue never appeared.

While the letter was being prepared, she made several changes in it, each one being an improvement on the former phrasing. After the letter had been finished, and even signed by her, she called me back again, and said, "Mr. Dickey, I must apologize to you for calling you so frequently, and troubling you so much, but won't you kindly bring that letter back to me?" I responded quickly and eagerly. Taking the letter, she glanced over it, drew her pencil through a word and replaced it with another. "There," she said with a triumphant smile, "that is exactly what I want to say." I took the letter from her to rewrite it, but before I could turn around, she reached forward and took it from my fingers, and placing it on her tablet she wrote the following words across the top of the letter: "Remember that the so-called human mind is expected to increase in wisdom until it disappears and Divine Mind is seen to be the only Mind."

"There," she said, "you may have that."

Mrs. Eddy realized that what was disturbing the Directors was the fact that she had changed her mind about something that they had considered quite important, but it seems that the changing of her mind was a privilege that our Leader reserved for herself, and she exercised it without any regard whatever for what had gone before, or what had been said. She declared, "Is a leader any less of a leader because she changes her mind?"

Then she said to me, "Mr. Dickey, people say I am change-able, — that I change my mind frequently, but when I do, it is always God that changes me. Sometimes I will be headed in one direction, like a weather vane, and will stay that way for several days. The next time you see me, I will have turned completely around and am going the other way, but in the meantime God has given me additional light and has led me to make the change." She said, "There have been times in working out a problem when I have not known just what step to take and finding it necessary to make a move of some sort, I have taken a step as nearly as I could in the right direction. Perhaps I would find out shortly that it was wrong, but this gave me a new point of view that I would not have had, had I not taken it as I did. I would not condemn myself, therefore, for what seemed a mistake, but would include it as part of the working out of the problem."

This thought, as expressed by our Leader, reminds me of an incident that took place some time afterward. The Committee on Publication for The Mother Church was preparing a very elabo-rate statement, showing the difference between Christian Science and a phase of Christian psychology, so-called. He sent his article to Mrs. Eddy for her approval. It passed through my hands and I took it to her, stating that the author wished to issue this in printed form for extensive circulation. Without a moment's hesitation she said, "No, this is not the thing for him to do. Tell him that I say to publish his article in one of the well-known daily newspapers and then await the result." I returned with her message to the Committee, and he remarked in a very loving way that he thought that Mrs. Eddy had not seen the situation from his point of view, and again expressed the hope that she would give her consent to his printing the article as he at first planned. When I brought his proposal to her again, she was most emphatic in her rejection of it. She said, "Mr. Dickey, he is trying to accomplish too much by one bound." Then she said to me, "Did you ever take such a long step that you fell to the ground?" I said, "Yes, Mother, I have." Then she asked, "Would it not have been better if you had taken two steps and retained your equilibrium? "It most certainly would," I replied. "Now," she continued, "this student is trying to do something at one step, which is not right, and I want him to do it as I first suggested. Please tell him again to publish this in a daily paper with a large circulation, and then leave it in the hands of God. He may never have to take another step." Again I communicated with the Committee, and he gladly accepted our Leader's proposal. The outcome was that the whole thing was settled as she predicted and nothing more was heard on the subject.

In reference to Mrs. Eddy's exactness in her statements of Science, and her requirement that those about her should be exact in their statements also, I recall that she put a high value on the verbal utterances of a practitioner and usually preferred that the mental workers should make their statements audibly. If there was any flaw in their work, she could instantly detect it and set the student on the right track. A carelessly worded treatment bespeaks a careless or indifferent thought, and any form of carelessness or inexactness of thought or expression was quickly corrected by our Leader. On one occasion when she was in need of encouragement I said to her, "Mother, you cannot have a return of an old belief." Up came the warning hand: "Don't put it that way," she said. "At one time I had a belief of excellent health, and your declaration, if carried out, would prevent me from expressing that belief of health, and that is what I am striving for." So I promised her I would never again be so careless.

What I should have said was, "diseased belief," and that error and mental malpractice could not cause the return of a diseased belief; or, "You cannot be made to suffer from a law of malpractice declaring that you shall have a return of an old belief of sickness."

Upon another occasion, when our Leader was having trouble with her throat, she called me in to help her. At once I saw that the belief was that there was a gathering of phlegm in her throat, and I began to declare that mortal mind could not create and that there was no such thing as phlegm in her throat. She stopped me at once and said, "Do not say that; there is a natural and normal secretion of phlegm in the throat, and if we declare against that, we are likely to interfere with the natural function of the glands of the throat." Then I changed my statement and said, "There is and there can be no such thing as an abnormal secretion of phlegm in your throat." This she approved.

I remember that on one occasion when a student in Mrs. Eddy's house was corrected because of an unscientific statement she made, Mrs. Eddy called her severely to account for her work in the presence of a number of others who were at that time under Mrs. Eddy's instruction. The student began to cry, and said, "I don't like you to talk to me like that; I want you to love me." Mrs. Eddy replied, "I do love you and that is the reason why I am talking to you in this way. If I did not love you, I would not take the time to correct you. It is because I want to have you be right and do right that I am correcting you," — and with that she dismissed her.

Chapter VIII

RELUCTANCE OF MRS. EDDY
TO CHANGE HER WRITINGS
IN RESPONSE TO CRITICISMS

By reason of the fact that much of what our Leader has written conflicts with the general thought of mankind, many people wrote letters to Mrs. Eddy suggesting that she change her books in various places and improve them by adopting the suggestions of her correspondents. Here again, our Leader's determination to be guided by divine Wisdom alone showed itself. One of her marked characteristics was that she rarely allowed anybody to criticize any of her writings, or call attention to what he considered an inappropriate expression. Even if there seemed good reason for a criticism, she was loath to accept it and in the majority of cases resisted what she considered to be interference from her critics. She wanted her book to be the product of her own thought and not a mixture of what mortal mind felt or believed on the subject. It seemed to me that this attitude of thought was really necessary because there were numerous instances when people thought Mrs. Eddy was making mistakes in her writings, with the result that she received more demands to change her statements than would ordinarily be sent to writers of books. Had she been any less wise than she was in her handling of this question, her book might indeed have presented much confused thought by reason of the interpolations of uninspired critics.

There were occasions, however, when Mrs. Eddy did make changes in *Science and Health* at the suggestion of others, but

these were the exception, and not the rule. One of the many proposals which came to her was a letter from her publisher, Mr. Allison
V. Stewart, advising Mrs. Eddy that a correspondent had called his
attention to her use of the word "hecatombs," where she speaks of
"hecatombs of gushing theories" on page 367 of *Science and
Health*. I confirmed Mr. Stewart's definition of the word by con-
sulting the dictionary, where it defined "hecatomb" as "a sacrifice
of the slaughter of one hundred cattle or oxen at the same time." It
seemed at that time to me that this criticism was well founded, and
when Mrs. Eddy received her mail on that day, I included this letter,
which had in it a recommendation that our Leader use some other
word, but the moment I presented it to her, her visage changed and
instantly she said, "No, Mr. Dickey, I will make no alteration in that
word. People do not always understand my sense of humor. This
statement is used in a sense of ridicule. The word conveys exactly
the sense I wish to present, namely, — that a great slaughter of
gushing theories, stereotyped borrowed speeches, and the doling
of arguments are but so many parodies on legitimate Christian
Science." Afterward, in further investigating the meaning of this
word, I found that a well-known dictionary defines it as "a great
slaughter." It was then quite clear to me that our Leader's version
was upheld and that no change should be made in the word.

A Christian Science healer, who was formerly a practising
physician, wrote me a letter in which he stated that Mrs. Eddy had
not employed the right use of the word "cicatrized" on page 162,
line 21, of *Science and Health*, where she formerly stated
"cicatrized joints have been made supple." He said "ankylosed"
was the proper word and no doubt this is what our Leader meant. I
showed the letter to her, and she demurred at making the change,
but after a careful inspection of the dictionary, she allowed the
change to be made. She explained to me that she had used the
word "cicatrized" purely from memory without investigating its real
meaning, and she expressed gratitude for having had this called to
her attention.

49

A letter received from a lady in England called attention to a statement made by Mrs. Eddy in *Miscellaneous Writings* in reply to an English critic. She referred to him as a "beer-bulged, surly censor," and my correspondent thought it was unkind for Mrs. Eddy to use the word "beer-bulged," as it seemed to her like employing an epithet, when Christian Scientists should express nothing but love. Mrs. Eddy did not like the tone of the letter, nor the suggestion contained therein, but nevertheless the criticism did appeal to our Leader and she revised the article, leaving out the word in question.

Chapter IX

CHANGES IN THE WRITINGS

Mrs. Eddy used to make slight changes from time to time in *Science and Health,* as Christian Scientists were aware. She was a constant student of her own writings, and after reading a passage, if it seemed to her that it could be illuminated or made plainer by some slight alteration she would make it. These alterations, like everything else that emanated from Mrs. Eddy's pen, were most carefully handled, and great pains were taken to see that everything was just as she expressed it.

During the first part of my stay with her these changes were handled by Mr. Frye, but later on they passed through my hands. Our Leader would first make the change in lead pencil in her book; then a letter was prepared to Mr. Stewart, her publisher, requesting that the change be made. This letter was signed by Mrs. Eddy, as her publisher would under no circumstances make any alteration in her books except in response to a direct request from her. The proposed change was then sent to the printer and a proof sheet made, which was in turn sent to our Leader for her approval. After this was obtained, the order was put through for a change in the plates, and when this was done, Mrs. Eddy was notified that the final arrangements were completed, and then the editions containing the change were issued. I am giving this detail in order that the reader may know how much care was exercised whenever a change was to be made in *Science and Health.*

Upon one occasion our Leader called me to her study and I found that she and Laura Sargent were discussing an alteration in

Science and Health that Mrs. Eddy had just proposed. They both seemed quite pleased with the change and asked me what I thought of it. I said at once that I thought it clarified the meaning of the text to me. The change was made at the top of page 503 of *Science and Health* in the chapter "Genesis." Our Leader had with her pencil erased the word "unfolding" in line 1, page 503, and substituted the word "reflection," and instead of the word "reflected" in the third line, she used the word "unfolding," making the text read: "This creation consists of the reflection of spiritual ideas and their identities, which are embraced in the infinite Mind and forever unfolding."

After expressing my pleasure at the contemplated change, I left the room and afterwards looked for this alteration in subsequent editions of the book, but for some reason, unknown to me, the change never appeared. This particular work was not at that time under my care, and it may be that our Leader decided later to leave the text as it stood, but whatever was done I am sure was with her sanction and approval.

No lesser degree of care was exercised in all articles prepared by Mrs. Eddy for publication. There were many letters received by her from students in the field, which she read with a great deal of pleasure. I found that in her isolated position she came in very little contact with the outside field, and only through the avenue opened by these letters to our Leader did she come in touch with the individual workers. These letters, usually expressing the gratitude of someone who had been healed or rescued from a critical situation in which mortal mind had placed the writer, were always read by Mrs. Eddy with pleasure and interest. If she wanted a letter published, she turned the page over and wrote "Eddy" across the back. Sometimes she would write, "Publish this," but these letters were always carefully scrutinized by her; whenever she wrote her name across the back or across the letter, it indicated that the editor was at liberty to use it in his make-up of the *Sentinel*.

One morning after she had called the class into her room, she opened *Science and Health* at random, to page 221, and began to read at line 1. In a moment she paused, looked up at the class smilingly and said, "Perhaps you will be interested to know that I am the woman who adopted that system." This was quite a surprise to us all. But she very quickly passed the incident by and made no further remarks in explanation of it. I learned afterward that in her first edition of *Science and Health*, referring to this same illustration, she used the editorial "We," thereby indicating that she herself was the person referred to. In subsequent editions, however, she spoke of "knowing a woman who when quite a child," and so forth. A short while after the above incident took place, she called me into her room and proceeded to change the text of *Science and Health* so that instead of "I knew a woman who when quite a child," and so on, it read, "I knew a person who when quite a child," and so forth. All through this page, 221, and the following page she changed the pronoun so that in each instance it referred to the person. Then with a very knowing smile she handed me these changes and asked me to send them to her publisher and have them executed in *Science and Health*. I saw clearly at once why she made the change; it was because she thought in telling five or six persons that she was the individual referred to, she had to a greater or lesser extent liberated this information in human thought and that it might become knowledge that it was she herself who was referred to. This did not suit her and she at once made the changes on these two pages, so as to turn the thought of mortal mind away from herself.

On one occasion Mrs. Eddy called me into her room and I found her considering a change in the title of her book, *Science and Health*. Instead of having it *Science and Health with Key to the Scriptures*, she proposed making it read, "Science and Health, Key to the Scriptures."

She asked me what I thought of the idea and if I understood the import of it. I told her that I did indeed, and that I thought it would be a splendid change as it would at once convey to people the thought that her whole book was the "key" which unlocked the Scriptures, and not chapters 15, 16, and 17, as would appear from the inscription "Key to the Scriptures" found on page 499 of her book as it stood at that time.

Mrs. Eddy was quite pleased with the idea and spoke favorably of it. She talked it over with her publisher and explained that she would like to make this change in the title of her book, provided it did not conflict in any way with her copyrights.

Mr. Stewart, her publisher at that time, made inquiry from Mrs. Eddy's Boston lawyers, and the word came back that they would not advise her to do this as it might materially affect the copyrights of her book.

Thus our Leader abandoned one of the inspired thoughts that came to her and which would have enlarged considerably the thought of all Christian Scientists regarding her book, *Science and Health*. I shall always look on the whole book as "Key to the Scriptures," as I am sure she desired that Christian Scientists should do.

On one occasion she was looking through the *Christian Science Hymnal*, where her poem "The Mother's Evening Prayer" is set to music. She made a change in the words "mother finds her home and far-off rest" by erasing "far-off" and inserting the word "heavenly" as it now reads. She asked me what I thought of the change. I told her that to me it conveyed a much better thought than as it was then written. I said that "her home and far-off rest" carried the impression that she had a long and toilsome way ahead of her. She said, "That is just the thing I want to get rid of."

I must confess that the words "heavenly rest" did not appeal to me immediately and I hesitated somewhat in replying to her question about what I thought of the words "heavenly rest." She noticed this hesitation in my manner and immediately her pencil was in action and she wrote the word "heavenly" as she had already designed, and in a determined way she said, "That's the word that shall go in."

At one time there went out by mistake to the field the impression that the first edition of *Science and Health* had been called in. In opening the mail one morning, I came upon a copy sent in by a woman responding to what she supposed was a call for the book, and inclosing a beautiful note. I carried both the package and the note in to Mrs. Eddy. She took the book in her hands, opened it, read a few lines, turned the leaves fondly, read again for a little, and as she did so I could see that past experiences were filling her thought. If ever you have seen a mother take down from a shelf or cupboard the first little shoes her baby wore, and fondly touch them with love in her eyes, you can imagine how Mrs. Eddy appeared when she looked at that book. At length she closed it slowly, gently, and placing it in my hand again, said with deepest feeling and tears in her eyes, "Take it, and put it away, Mr. Dickey, — no one will ever know what it has cost me to write that book."

Chapter X

THE TWILIGHT HOUR
"AWAKE THOU THAT SLEEPEST"

If our Leader had any favorite hour in the day, I think it was after the evening meal, at twilight, when she loved to sit quietly in her room and gaze from her window at the lengthening shadows. She invited me to come in at this hour whenever my work permitted me to do so, and on these occasions she always extended a greeting hand and asked me to sit down beside her. Often she told me many things of interest in her life. We had bright electric lights installed on the gateposts where her driveway entered the street, and she would sometimes make remarks about the vehicles that passed her residence. It might seem that these were idle thoughts for the Leader of a great Movement, and that such commonplace things as the traffic that passed her door could be of no possible interest to the Discoverer and Founder of Christian Science, but when we consider that Mrs. Eddy virtually lived in three rooms, and seldom, if ever, gave any thought to the simple activities of the world about her, she might be excused for indulging in such trifles. She used to sit in her chair beside her desk, with her own room darkened so that she could the better see what was going on outside. At her elbow on her desk was a tiny clock with a small electric light in front of it so that when she pushed a button, the dial would be illuminated and she could tell the hour. Our Leader retired early and it was seldom that she was not in bed by nine o'clock. The watchers were ready to take up their work at that time, and the one who covered from nine to eleven usually sat in her study outside of her bedroom door.

One evening, shortly after Mrs. Eddy had retired, Mrs. Sargent came to my door in great trepidation, informing me that she had found Calvin Frye unconscious on the lounge in his room and that she had been unable to arouse him. I hurriedly accompanied her and found Mr. Frye stretched on the lounge in a most uncomfortable attitude, speechless and eyes closed, apparently breathless and with no pulse or indication of life whatever. We continued our efforts to arouse him but with no success. We called to him, shook him, and used every means at our command. Finally another worker came in and united his efforts with ours, but we could gain no response of any kind in our efforts to call Mr. Frye back. We hesitated about letting our Leader know of his condition, but we saw that inasmuch as we were making no headway, we must inform her of the circumstances.

This was done by Mrs. Sargent. Mrs. Eddy was in bed, but she hurriedly rang her bell for her maid and started to arise and dress herself, when she was seized with a sudden determination, and dropping back into bed she said, "I cannot wait to dress. Bring him to me." Mrs. Sargent said, "But, Mother, he is unconscious. We cannot rouse him." She said, "Bring him to me at once." On receiving this instruction, the one who had come to our aid lifted the senseless form of Calvin Frye and placed him in a low rocking-chair. Then we dragged him around through the hall, through Mrs. Eddy's study, into her bedroom. She sat up in bed with a shawl or some kind of a robe over her shoulders, and we drew Mr. Frye right up to her side where she could both touch and speak to him. It was an interesting moment. The workers stood around the small room and watched the proceedings. Our Leader reached out her hand and placed it upon Mr. Frye's shoulder and addressed him in a loud voice. "Calvin, Calvin, wake up. It is Mother who is calling you. Wake up, Calvin, this Cause needs you, Mother needs you, and you must not leave. Calvin, Calvin, wake up. Disappoint your enemies. You shall not go. I need you here. Disappoint your enemies, Calvin, and awake." All this time Mr. Frye's head was hanging limp on his shoulder. I had hold of the back of the rocking chair in which we had placed him to steady him. I placed my hand on his head to lift it up. Mrs. Eddy instantly stopped me and said, "Do not touch him. Leave him entirely to me." Again, she repeated her calls to him to arouse himself and remain with her. It was now something like half an hour since Calvin had first been found, and while those who were looking on at our Leader's efforts to arouse him, had not the slightest doubt that she would succeed in awakening him, yet the time seemed to pass without any appreciable response to her work. This did not discourage her. She redoubled her efforts and fairly shouted to Mr. Frye her commands that he awake. In a moment he raised his head and drew a long, deep breath. After this his respiration became regular and he was restored to consciousness. The first words he uttered were, "I don't want to stay. I want to go." Mrs. Eddy paused in her efforts and turning her gaze to the workers around the room, said, "Just listen to that." She again turned to Mr. Frye and in her commanding tones insisted that he awake and remain here.

Never shall I forget the picture that was before us in that small bedroom, the light shining on the half-scared faces of the workers, and our Leader's intense determination to keep Mr. Frye with her. I had heard of similar occasions when rumors had reached the workers in the field that at different times our Leader had restored prominent students to life after experiences of this kind, but of this incident I was an eye-witness, and from the very first my attention was not diverted for one second from what was going on, and I am simply relating this event exactly as it occurred.

It had been rumored that Mrs. Eddy's power of healing was lost, but those who were present on this occasion have a different story to tell. Our Leader rose to the occasion like a giant, and in commanding tones she demanded that her servant should live, and he responded. When Mr. Frye became fully conscious, she turned him over to one of the workers who remained with him through the night. The next morning he was about his accustomed duties. Not one in the house, that I know of, said anything to Mr. Frye concerning his experience. We do not know whether he realized how far he had gone or whether, indeed, he knew of the work that had been done for him. No questions were asked him as we felt it would not be well to recite the experience to him, but the fact remains that Calvin Frye had passed through what mortal mind calls "death," and the grave had been cheated of its victim by our Leader's quick and effective work.

Chapter XI

LEADERSHIP AND DEVOTION
TO HER CAUSE

Frequently our Leader was called upon to make a decision of great importance at a moment's notice that would perhaps affect the future of her Cause for years. She seemed rarely to weigh in her thought what the consequence of her action might be. Her sole desire was to get the Divine leading and follow that unhesitatingly. Often the reasons for which our Leader took action in certain directions were not clear to the workers about her. It would seem as if the reason advanced by her was a poor one and not worthy of the action she was taking. This, of course, was mortal mind's analysis of her work, and if she were acting from a spiritual impulse, it is not at all surprising that her reasons would not appeal to the judgment of onlookers. It always turned out, however, that her action was right, regardless of the reason assigned, which convinced those who were familiar with her work that her judgment was unerring in every detail, and that in following the direction of divine Wisdom, she never made a mistake. Often I heard her say with great impressiveness that in over forty years of church leadership, she had not made a mistake, a record that is most truly remarkable.

A story is told of Charles M. Schwab, the steel magnate, who was reared under the tutelage of Andrew Carnegie. One day, the story goes, when Mr. Schwab was Carnegie's chief lieutenant, he described to his superior some action he had taken and then started to explain why he had taken it. "Oh, never mind the reason,

Charlie," Carnegie broke in, "what you do is always right, but your reasons for it are always wrong."

Mrs. Eddy's ideas of church government differed greatly from those of the general run of mankind. She knew that her Church, established as it was under Divine direction, would incur the hatred and opposition of every known form of religion, which has been evolved according to the wisdom of man. In order to be perpetuated, her Church must necessarily follow Divine inspiration and not be the product of legal enactments or worldy-wise evolutions. She told me that every government, every organization, every institution of whatever kind or nature, to be successful, must have one responsible head.

This is why she placed herself at the head of her own Church, because mortal mind could not be trusted to conduct it. This is why she did away with First Members, and later Executive Members, for to place enactments of holy inspiration in the hands of groups of individuals was to incur the possibility of the Divine idea being lost sight of, and human wisdom taking its place. This is also why she reduced the authority of the conduct of The Mother Church into the narrowest possible compass. Indeed, she told me, with pathos and earnestness, that if she could find one individual, who was spiritually equipped, she would immediately place him at the head of her church government. Asking me to take a pencil she slowly dictated the following, as I wrote it down: "I prayed God day and night to show me how to form my Church, and how to go on with it. I understand that He showed me, just as I understand He showed me Christian Science, and no human being ever showed me Christian Science. Then I have no right or desire to change what God has directed me to do, and it remains for the Church to obey it. What has prospered this Church for thirty years will continue to keep it."

It was her child, her offspring; and her constant concern, day and night, was what was to become of this Cause. Those of her followers who were present in her home can testify to her anxious thought in this direction. On several occasions, when she was trying to get her followers to see the import of this and what it meant, she would say, with a gesture of despair, "What is to become of this Cause?" And again, when troubled about the future of the Cause she would say, "If error can do this to me, what is it going to do to you?" She saw the possibility of future attacks of mortal mind upon her beloved Church, and her constant anxiety was for its preservation and future unfoldment. She told me that she had constantly watched the growth of this Church as would a parent the development of its offspring. She said that in all things while she was the Leader of the Christian Science Movement, she actually felt the needs of the Movement in her body just as the mother of a young infant would feel the needs of the infant and supply them. Instantly, detecting that I did not receive the full import of what she was telling me, she explained herself by saying that the mother of a young babe always knew by the condition of her breast when her child needed nourishment, and she said she also felt the same way in regard to the needs of the Christian Science Movement. The needs of her Church were frequently met through the enactment of some By-law, which, though it startled the Christian Science field, yet it seemed to be the imperative demand of Wisdom made upon our Leader. At times these decisions were arrived at after long nights of prayer and struggle.

There is no question that the By-law abolishing the Communion Service of The Mother Church came under this category. Our Leader had been suffering intensely for several days before this By-law came out, and even when she dictated to me the words included in it, she was lying on the lounge wrestling with a malicious attack of unusual severity. I took the proposed By-law, as she dictated it, to my desk and after transcribing it, I returned with it immediately to her room and was overjoyed to find her seated at her desk, wreathed in smiles, pursuing her regular work with her usual vigor. I saw that something out of the ordinary had taken place and afterward I learned from Mr. Frye that on many occassions, when our Leader instituted improvements for her Church government, her action had been accompanied by severe manifestations such as appeared in the present instance, and yet not one word of complaint passed her lips. She was willing to take the suffering if she could only succeed in obeying the voice of God.

Not long after this, when she was wrestling with what seemed to be a physical disturbance, I was trying to help her and in talking over the situation with her, I said, "Mother, you cannot be made to feel the effect of mortal mind thought and mortal mind cannot make you feel its argument." At that time she was lying down with closed eyes, but as soon as I made the statement, "mortal mind can't make you feel its argument," she looked up, and raising her hand in warning said, "Don't say that, Mr. Dickey." Then she went on in her loving and quiet way to explain that when she was able to feel what mortal mind had in thought, it enabled her to do that thing which was most helpful to the Cause of Christian Science. This, I think, exemplified the loving, self-sacrificing thought of our Leader. She was willing to endure the sufferings mortal mind imposed upon her, for thereby she was enabled to take some action that would be helpful to her Cause. How much we all owe to this dear soul, who thus offered herself as a perpetual sacrifice for the good of humanity, we may never know. "But he was wounded for our transgressions, he was bruised for our iniquities: the chastisement of our peace was upon him; and with his stripes we are healed." (Isaiah 53:5)

At the time when our Leader was compelled to live in two of her attic rooms at Chestnut Hill, she was looking forward to her return to her own apartments on the second floor. I remember how pleased she was when I told her a few days before that she would be in her new rooms by the following Saturday. There was much to be done, but every member of the household was working

63

eagerly to bring about the desired event, and on Saturday, March 14, upon returning from her drive, she was duly esconced in the new apartment. She was greatly pleased with the modification of the size of the room, the additional stairway to the third floor, and the new elevator, which dropped her immediately to the *portecochre* where she took her carriage.

In an earlier chapter I referred to the fact that I learned much while arranging the furniture, pictures, and ornaments under Mrs. Eddy's personal direction. It was not like arranging the furniture of an ordinary room. Here was where the most wonderful woman that the world has ever produced, was to spend her time and thought in the direction and government of the greatest Christian Movement that was ever known. I could see clearly the working of divine Principle, even in the arrangement of the ornaments on her mantel. There was a reason for everything, and it was all worked out so beautifully and harmoniously that the experience was most uplifting to me, while at the same time it gave me the opportunity of getting closer in thought to our revered Leader than I had done before.

In my own home, when I hung a picture, I used a simple device which I had invented that I called a picture stick. It consisted of flat hooks on the end of a long stick, which enabled me to set the picture hook on the end of the stick, and immediately place it where desired. It could be taken down and put back with such ease that the labor of picture hanging was reduced to a minimum. This little device pleased Mrs. Eddy very much and drew forth from her the remark that after all, it was Mind that hung the picture.

One of the last pictures placed in the room was a remarkably well-executed one entitled "The Return from the Crucifixion." It represented the return of the women from the cross. It showed the beloved disciple ascending the steps of his home, sustaining the drooping form of the mother of Jesus, whom the latter had entrusted to John's care. The faces of the group shown in the picture, with the exception of Jesus' mother, were anxiously turned toward a hill beyond the walls of Jerusalem, where silhouetted against the sky appeared three crosses, which stood as mute witnesses of the dreadful day's experience. After leaving Mrs. Eddy's study, I was recalled in a few minutes, and, pointing with one hand to the picture just described and placing the other on her breast, she said in a voice deep and earnest in its subdued tones, " Mr. Dickey, I think you had better remove that picture. It suggests too much for me. Won't you kindly put another in its place?" This I did, and removed the offending picture to the hall on the second floor outside of her room, where it remains to this day.

Later in the evening, about half past eight, she called for me, and taking both my hands in hers she said, "Now dear, if you keep your watch tonight, you may go to The Mother Church tomorrow morning." I said, "Mother, I really don't care to go to The Mother Church." She said, "I would like you to go because I think you would enjoy it." I assured her that I would much prefer to remain where she was and that I could learn much more by hearing the few words dropped from her lips than I could by listening to a Lesson Sermon read in The Mother Church. This decision seemed to please her, and she said, "Very well, Mr. Dickey, let that be as you will."

At this time there were four mental workers in the house, in addition to Mr. Frye, and the hours of the night were divided into four separate watches, so-called. The first watch was from 9:00 to 11:00 P.M.; the next, from 11:00 to 1:00 A.M.; the next, from 1:00 to 3:00; and then, from 3:00 until 5:00 in the morning. These watches were assigned to different mental workers, and their task was to counteract the malicious evil influence of mortal mind directed towards our Leader and her establishment during their two hours. When a watch was kept, or in other words, when the mental worker was successful in freeing our Leader from attacks during that time, she always knew it, and the one keeping the watch was commended the next day. If the watch was not kept, and they were far more frequently not kept than kept, a corresponding rebuke was administered to the one who failed. This may look like strenuous work, but be it remembered that no one in that household worked half so hard as our Leader did, and we were there to do this work and rejoiced when it was accomplished. It was a constant battle for our Leader even to live in order that she might devote her time and energies to the conduct and welfare of the great Cause, which had grown up as a result of her foundational work.

On many occasions all the workers were called in and admonished because of their seeming inability to meet the prevailing conditions. It was our Leader's custom, when she went to her study in the morning, to first open the Bible and read whatever appeared on the page before her. This was apparently done at random, and yet she seemed directed in this work so that the reference on most occasions was particularly fitting to the subject under discussion. One passage especially seemed to thrust itself forward on these occasions. It was Matthew 24:43, "But know this, that if the goodman of the house had known in what watch the thief would come, he would have watched, and would not have suffered his house to be broken up."

One morning after she read this passage to us, our Leader said, "We must watch and pray. Prayer means desire. We can have words without the desire, but that is not prayer. Prayer must have no selfishness in it. Hanging pictures and arranging furniture, for another's pleasure is unselfishness, and to the degree that it is unselfish, it is like God. To be able to dress and adorn one's self beautifully is selfishness. To do it for another is unselfishness." Then she quoted lines 30 and 31, page 192 of *Science and Health*.

Afterward, she told us that a student had been sending her fresh eggs, which he wanted to furnish her free. "Do you want me to do a wrong thing by taking your eggs without paying you for them; or, will you do right by accepting from me what is just?"

At one time, when we were all called into her room, she said, "Mr. Dickey, have you sent a certain letter to be published?" "No," I replied. "Do not send it," she said. "This matter of students coming here for a few days and then going away and proclaiming what wonderful things they have learned is a menace to the Cause. When they learn anything, they stay here. They are not sent away. When they are sent away and give out the idea that they know so much, they are over-reaching themselves, and deceiving others. Where all students have failed is in not knowing how to handle animal magnetism. If we don't break the belief that mesmerism has power, we are still the victims of mesmerism, and it is handling us. Now then, the main point is to keep your watch. Keep your watch. Jesus said, Could ye not watch with me one hour?" (Matthew 26:40.) Then again she quoted, "'If the good man of the house had known in what watch the thief would come, he would have watched.'" (Matthew 24:43.) "If you can defeat the mesmerist in this, you can defeat him in all things," she continued. "He boasts that he can make a law for you, six months ahead, and then work to cover every hour in the night. You must break their supposed laws that they can produce suffering asleep or awake." After a long talk and many illustrations and admonitions, we were dismissed. We were all recalled in a few moments and asked, "Now what is the great necessity I have been impressing on you?" I replied, "Demonstration." Others said something else. She said, "No, you are all wrong. You have missed the importance of the lesson I have just given you. I felt it and called you back to show you your ignorance. The lesson is this, — keep your watch." Then we were dismissed. Shortly we were called back again, and she said, "What I have to meet, you will all have to meet, now or again. Therefore, know that the mesmerist cannot afflict either you or me with erroneous beliefs." We all solemnly promised to keep our watch. Our Leader responded, "Amen." During the course of the talk, she said, "If you will keep your watch, I shall be a well woman. If you stay here until you learn to handle animal magnetism, I will make healers out of you. I had to do it, and did it for forty years, and you must do it. You must rise to the point where you can destroy the belief in mesmerism, or you will have no Cause. It tried to overcome me for forty years and I withstood it all. Now it has gotten to the point where the students must take up this work and meet animal magnetism. I cannot do it for you. You must do it for yourselves, and unless it is done, the Cause will perish and we will go along another 1900 years with the world sunk into the blackest night. Now will you rouse yourselves? You have all the power of God with you to conquer this lie of mesmerism. The workers in the field are not healing because they are not meeting animal magnetism which says they cannot heal." Then she turned to each one and said, "Will you keep your watch?" They all answered, "Yes." She turned to me and said, "Mr. Dickey, will you keep your watch?" I said, "Yes, Mother, I will." She leaned forward in her chair and took my hand in hers, and I knew from the pressure, as well as the look she gave, she knew I would keep my watch. In explanation she said, "To keep your watch doesn't only mean to be awake at that hour and be working mentally. It means to do the work and succeed in breaking the mesmerism for the two hours assigned. If you don't succeed, you haven't kept your watch."

I have been trying to record many of our Leader's words as nearly verbatim as possible, but I am unable to record more than a small portion of her sayings. The one thing she has impressed on her students is that they must handle animal magnetism and defeat the mental murderer and mental assassin who are working to defeat this Cause.

At another time she said, "There is a new form of sin or malpractice that has been revealed to me that nobody has ever discovered before, and that is that evil is trying to produce sudden death in sleep. The serpent typifies evil, and the moccasin snake will lie right beside a person who is awake, and never touch him, but as soon as he falls asleep, he will attack."

Chapter XII

CHILDHOOD EXPERIENCES

Mrs. Eddy told me much of an interesting nature about her childhood home. She was the youngest of six children, who were as follows: Samuel, born in 1808; Albert, in 1810; George, in 1812; Abigail, in 1816; Martha, in 1819; and Mary, in 1821. The children were reared in a most religious atmosphere. The clergy were always welcomed at their home, and family Bible reading and prayer were a daily exercise.

Mrs. Eddy's mother, Mrs. Mark Baker, had a neighbor who was a most devout and pious woman. Her name was Sarah Gualt, and she and Mrs. Baker used frequently and regularly to meet and talk over religious matters and pray together audibly. During these meetings Mrs. Baker many times told her neighbor, Mrs. Gualt, that she felt herself to be a most wicked woman because of the strange thoughts she had regarding her youngest child, which was yet unborn. (Mrs. Eddy related the circumstance of her birth which was similar to that referred to in Hebrews 11:11.) She told Mrs. Gualt that she could not keep her thought away from the strong conviction that this child was holy and consecrated and set apart for wonderful achievements, even before her birth. She said, "I know these are sinful thoughts for me to entertain, but I cannot shake them off." Then these two devout women would talk the question over and pray together, asking God's direction and blessing on this subject.

When Mrs. Eddy was still a child, her elder brothers frequently quarreled among themselves, as brothers sometimes will, and even went so far as to use their fists in settlement of their difficulties. These altercations greatly disturbed their little sister, Mary, and whenever they quarreled, she industriously undertook to bring about a reconciliation between the disputants. She told me that she never failed in these endeavors. When the breach seemed wide and the brothers were far apart in thought, this would not dismay her in the slightest. She went resolutely from one to the other, and back and forth, she carried their messages until they met and asked each other's forgiveness. She would say, "George, you love Sam, don't you?" He would say, "Yes," and then she would say, "You don't want to quarrel, do you?" George would invariably reply, "No." She would then go to Sam and say, "You love your brother, George, don't you?" "Yes, Mary, I do," he would answer. "Then you don't want to hold any ill-will, do you?" "I certainly don't." "Then, why don't you tell him so?" In that way this little child persisted in bringing the brothers together and settling their quarrels.

This inborn proclivity, which asserted itself thus in childhood, clung to her throughout her after years, and quarrels or misunderstandings of any kind were always abominations to her. Whenever questions in dispute came under her observation, she said she never failed to effect a reconciliation.

There were many incidents of an unusual nature which attended Mrs. Eddy's childhood. Her father used to attempt to break her will, but in this she was invariably protected by her mother who would say, Mark, you must not antagonize Mary. You know she is always right and I cannot allow you to be overbearing or cruel to her. Mrs. Eddy told me that even when a child, she had an indomitable will and this continued throughout all her future years. It was recognized and respected by her parents, especially her mother, who always remembered her early prayers and experiences concerning the unusual thoughts she had attending Mary's birth.

The determined quality of thought on her part to abide by

her own sincere convictions was shown a few years later, when she united with the Congregational Church, where she refused to change her theological views, even though it might result in her being left out of church fellowship. She stoutly maintained that she would take her chance of spiritual safety with her brothers and sisters, none of whom had professed religion, but she could not change her creedal doubts. In after years this strong determination on our Leader's part stood her well in hand, protecting and defending the Cause she espoused. A person without such strong conviction and forceful determination could never have stood the opposition and antagonism of those who were opposed to her revelations. A weak and vacillating individual never becomes a successful reformer.

The question has often been asked, "Why was Christian Science discovered by a woman?" Since my acquaintance with Mrs. Eddy, it has always been perfectly plain and clear to me why it must be that a woman should give birth to this new religion and stand and defend it against the world. Is it not evident that throughout the whole animal kingdom the female of the species has always been the defender of the offspring? Hunters of wild animals much prefer to meet the father than to encounter a lioness or tigress who is protecting her young. A mother bear with cubs is a much more dangerous antagonist than Bruin himself. The instinct of motherhood and readiness to protect her offspring have been strong characteristics in our Leader's whole career. I doubt if any man could have been found who would have stood and defended this Movement as she has done. Thus we see that from early childhood the qualities necessary for the protection of this great Cause seemed to be inherent in Mrs. Eddy's thought.

An incident illustrating Mary Baker's unusual mental development, as a child, is shown in the following. The family had a dog in the house named "Ben," and when they were assembled in the sitting room, the dog was made to understand that he must always lie under the table. Sometimes he would disregard this injunction and would come out and sit before the fire with the family. Mrs. Eddy said she found out that by mentally addressing the dog, he would obey her without her speaking a word aloud. When she saw that Ben was in for trouble, because of his presence in the room, she would mentally say, "Ben, go under the table and lie down," and immediately the dog would rise and walk under the table and lie down. This, she said, occurred many, many times, and was one of the incidents of her childhood which she always kept to herself.

Her father seemed to know that she was an unusual child and that even when very young, she seemed to possess healing qualities. She told me that once while her elder brother, Sam, was chopping wood, the axe glanced and inflicted a severe wound in his leg. He was put in bed and remained there for many days, the wound apparently refusing to heal. When the family were about to despair of the boy's recovery, Mary's father picked her up and approaching the bed, he turned aside the covers and gently placed Mary's hand over the wound, holding it there for some little time. From that moment Sam's leg grew rapidly well, while Mary for several days suffered with a high fever and delirium, as a result of this experience. Her extreme sensitiveness to the sufferings of others began even in childhood, and thus in a way seemed to forecast the future that lay before her.

When Mary Baker was still a very young child, perhaps not over eight years of age, she was a close and devoted student of the Bible. Her mother used to read to her the story of Daniel and how he prayed three times a day with his window open toward Jerusalem. This made such an impression upon the child that she also decided to pray every day to God, not only three times, but seven times. She knelt before God and poured out her little soul to Him in prayer, and in order to be free and uninterrupted in this devotional work, she would leave the house and retire to the wood-shed, where she could be alone, and there she knelt and prayed seven times, daily. In order that she might not fail in fulfilling her obligation, she kept a small piece of chalk and marked on the side of the shed each time, so that she might not miss even one of the seven prayers she had obligated herself to make. As she related this incident to me, her whole face lightened with a joyous expression and she said, "Just think of that little tot praying seven times a day and making a record of each prayer so that she would not miss one! Did ever you see or hear of such a thing!" I assured her that I had not, and as I talked with her about it and expressed my pleasure in hearing of the incident, I said, "That is very characteristic of the devotion that many of us have seen you display in your work as Leader of The Christian Science Movement." She replied, "Yes, I have always been devoted to what I had in hand, and considered that everything I did to forward this Movement was an obligation to God that had to be sincerely kept."

Another childhood incident, which had already been told me a number of times before I learned it from Mrs. Eddy's lips, proves interesting enough to bear repeating. She told me that on cold winter nights, when the little pigs in the sty outside were squealing, she asked her mother's consent to go out to the sty and sing the little pigs to sleep. At first, her mother objected, but having learned, as she herself said, never to interfere with anything Mary wished to do, she gave her consent. Putting a shawl over her head, the little girl went out and crouching near the sty sang to the little pigs until they stopped their squealing and went to sleep, and as she sang, she prayed, and her efforts never failed.

On page 95 of *Miscellaneous Writings*, Mrs. Eddy refers to the fact that her life was always attended by phenomena of an uncommon order. This recalls an incident she related to me on one occasion. She told me in detail all the circumstances connected with the statement she makes in *Retrospection and Introspection*, page 8, under the caption, Voices not our own. After finishing she said, "I have never told to any one the circumstances that followed my answer, Speak, Lord, for thy servant heareth, but I will tell you what took place." She then related in a voice filled with awe, that when she made the reply, a most unusual phenomenon took place. Her body was lifted entirely from the bed, on which she lay, to a height, it seemed to her, of about one foot. Then it was laid gently back on the bed. This was repeated three times. As a child she was afraid to tell the circumstance to anybody, but she pondered it deeply in her heart and thought of it many years afterward, when she was demonstrating the nothingness of matter and that the claim of the human body was a myth.

The foregoing narratives of incidents in the life of our Leader are but some of those related to me by Mrs. Eddy during the memorable twilight hours when we sat and talked together in her study at Chestnut Hill.

For further information regarding Christian Science:
Write   The Bookmark
Post Office Box 801143
Santa Clarita, CA 91380
Call   1-800-220-7767
Visit our website: www. thebookmark.com